Quickstart to Tango

by Jeff Allen

Q Q S Publications

Cranston, RI

Allen, Jeffrey H. a/k/a Allen, Jeff   1949 -
Quickstart to Tango
1. Dancing   2. Ballroom Dancing   3. Tango 4. Social Activity 5. Dancesport I. Title

Published by:
Q Q S Publications
1315 New London Avenue
Cranston, RI 02920

Library of Congress Catalog Card Number: 97-91693

International Standard Book Number: 0-9654423-2-2

First Edition, 1998
1-2-3-4-5-6-7-8-9-10-11-12
Printed in the United States of America

ABOUT THE AUTHOR

Jeff Allen is a graduate of the University of Rhode Island who has been self-employed since 1972. Jeff's interest in Social & Ballroom Dancing began in 1960 with social dance classes in the Providence, RI area. By the late 70's Jeff's interest in competitive dancing began to consume all of his free time. At that time Disco dancing and Disco Night Club competition were the main thrusts of his dance activity. These dance competitions were held all over the New England and New York areas where Jeff won thousands of dollars competing. The Disco craze soon subsided and competitive Ballroom & Latin Dancing piqued Jeff's interest. He began competing in national and international dance competitions. Jeff turned professional in July of 1984 after winning the Gold closed level at the North American Championships. In that same year Jeff began traveling to Montreal, Quebec, a Mecca of Ballroom Dancing, for teacher training and competitive dancing. This journey continued every four weeks for 3 years. Jeff finished in 4th place in the Canadian Provincial Basic & Standard Professional Latin Championships, won the New England Professional American Smooth Championships, finished 2nd in the Rising Star Closed Latin North American Championships, and was a finalist in the Eastern United States Championships in both the Professional Open American Smooth and Professional Open International Latin Divisions. His interest in Argentine Tango developed when training in Montreal during 1986. Fascinated by this form of Tango, he took a bold step and added elements of the Argentine style to his professional American Tango choreography. Today all top competitors in the American Smooth divisions use Argentine Tango to add drama to the American style. Jeff's greatest pride is the more than 30 Top Teacher Awards he has won and having kept his position consistently in the list of the Top 75 teachers in North America. This was done while competing Professionally and performing an average of more than one show per week.

Jeff holds Associate credentials with the Imperial Society of Teachers of Dance and the Pan American Teachers Association. In addition to this text, *Quickstart To Tango©*, Jeff has completed the 2nd edition of *Quickstart to Social Dancing©*, and is completing the 3rd of eleven books in the *Quickstart Series*, called *Quickstart To Swing©*. Jeff continues to offer the highest standard in teaching beginner and advanced students including teachers and professional performers.

An Important Note to the Reader

Maximum benefit will be achieved if the user reads the entire text before beginning his lessons. In this way you will be best mentally prepared to begin. The special lay-flat binding will keep the pages from flipping and will increase the life of the book. The student will observe the logical and cumulative flow of the lesson structure and presentation starting with stationary and then the moving exercises which will actually form the foundation for each dance. The actual text can be read in a few hours. The text and photos have been designed for easy visual and physical use. This text is primarily concerned with two of the **social** forms of Tango danced in North America. There are over 30 patterns in each of two Tango styles addressed in this book. **Although they are both classified as Tango, they are really very different dances.** The technique in general and specific to either the American or Argentine Tango will take the reader well beyond the choreographical bounds presented in Quickstart To Tango. Mr. Allen is available to answer any of your questions regarding this book. His readers may contact him through the QQS Publications' Website:

http://home.earthlink.net/~dancebook/

or email directly to :

dancebook@earthlink.net

Thank you for purchasing *Quickstart to Tango* © and please enjoy yourselves.

ACKNOWLEDGMENTS

To **Whitney**,

I have learned about myself through you and your love and have grown as a result. We complete each other and make our lives full. I love you for that. 2/23/98

To My Children - **Joshua**, **Bethanie**, **& Jessica**,

You three are extraordinarily talented and beautiful. It is a blessing to be your Dad. I know that your lives will be enriched even as you have and continue to enrich mine.

To my teaching mentor -**Pierrette Chartier** of Montreal,

Without trying you taught me the art of teaching dance as you epitomize what a teacher should be. You always shared your knowledge without reserve in a loving and compassionate way.

To **Diesel**,

You give constant unconditional love and companionship and require nothing except some simple food, a walk outside, and a ball to catch. Thank you for being there to calm me and make me laugh while writing this book.

The Index of this text has been prepared by Whitney A. Brown

WARNING –DISCLAIMER

This book is designed to provide information in regard to the subject matter covered. It is sold with the understanding that neither the publisher nor the author intends the reader to engage in any physical activity that can be construed as out of the ordinary. There is no intent by the publisher and author to cause the reader to unduly exert or strain himself physically. Each movement covered by this text is considered by the publisher and author to be well within the realm of ordinary and normal movement for a healthy human. A healthy human being has no physical problems concerning motor skills, or the use of joints or muscles. Should you experience pain from any movement in general or upon beginning to use this text, you should seek the advice of your physician before continuing. Do not exceed any limitations of movement your physician suggests.

This book is designed to provide the most basic and simple dance lessons and dance level experience. *Quickstart to Tango©* is the very beginning of your Tango dancing experience. It is very suitable for those who just want to get by. Anyone who expects to dance very well must be prepared to invest a lot of time and money. We have two objectives in using "Quickstart to Tango.©" The first objective is to get you out on the dance floor as soon as possible and looking as good as possible. The second is to provide you with a dance resource and reference guide for your continuing dance education.

Every effort has been made to make this manual as complete within its scope and as accurate as possible. However, there may be mistakes, both typographical and in content. Therefore, this text should be used only as a general guide and not as the ultimate source of dance information.

The purpose of this text is to educate and entertain. The author and QQS Publications have neither liability nor responsibility to any person or entity with respect to any loss or damage caused, or alleged to be caused, directly or indirectly by the information contained in this book.

If you do not wish to be bound by the above, you may return this book to the publisher, in marketable condition, for a full refund.

Table of Contents

Introduction To Tango

America is a melting pot of people, cultures, and traditions. I have presented two forms of Tango that are really different dances. However, as with all cultural things in America we adapt to trends and changes. The American style of Tango has room within its progressive and powerful nature for momentary soft and passion filled interludes found in the Argentine style of Tango. This then can become a time for conversing with your partner during the dance!   I love both styles of Tango and present them in one book for your cultural growth and physical enjoyment.

Tango as a social partner dance is a means of recreation and enjoyment for a lifetime. There are no sociological, chronological, or economic boundaries in tango dancing. When you are out for the evening dancing with your partner, you are spending your time wisely. Anyone would be hard pressed to find another activity which depends so heavily on the synchronized physical and mental cooperation of a man and a woman. Tango requires this togetherness and rewards us with so much more. Tango portrays passion, excitement, love, anger, romance, and every other sensation between a man and a woman. Tango dancing is both theatrical and eccentric. It is the chosen dance for many leading men and women of live theater and on the silver screen. Tango is not a difficult dance. Therefore these non-dancing actors have actually produced rather good interpretations of Tango. One of my favorite quotations regarding the ease with which Tango can be accomplished is, Al Pacino's line in the Tango scene in the movie Scent Of A Woman. "Tango is not like life, my dear. There are no mistakes in Tango.......If you get tangled up, you just tango on." You will find the choreographical content of the Tango between Al Pacino and Gabrielle Anwar throughout the covers of this text.

Dancing satisfies the emotional, the artistic, the intellectual, the physical, and even the competitive spirit of its participants.

Once you begin Quickstart To Tango you will find learning to dance using my very simple method will be fun and most definitely intoxicating. Without a doubt you will experience the need to go past the contents of this book. Your objective at this time should be learning enough to go out with your partner and enjoying yourselves. Maybe you will be the one couple that everyone talks about when the last note of music has been played. Don't laugh; it could happen! Tango is happening everywhere around us, Tango clubs are forming, and brides and grooms are now choosing to do a Tango as their first dance.

This book has been written in a very simple and functional form for easy use by my readers. Lessons are included in my first book, Quickstart To Social Dancing and can be referred to for an approach to body movement. Each new figure will have a full chart followed by a comprehensive description of each step number. Once you become familiar with a step in a recurring form, pattern, or technique, your learning curve will accelerate. I have constructed my Quickstart program so that there will be little or nothing for you, my student, to figure out or interpret. Exactly what you need to know to begin dancing either style of Tango will be included in this book.

You will soon see that only a minute segment of our population has really taken a dance lesson beyond the level of this book. Believe me, the experts are very few and far between. If indeed there are expert dancers where you find yourself doing the Tango they know what is involved in learning to dance and will probably be of assistance to you. The intimidation exist only within you. Just go out there and expect to really enjoy yourselves.

When I begin to train a couple in person, I suggest that the key to expeditious learning will be the time they spend in rehearsal, practice, and repetition. With this book you will be able to learn at your own pace and comfort level. Each dance figure in this book will become easier to learn because of the cumulative method presented.

In the first few exercises you will learn things like learning to walk like a Tango dancer's partner which includes the characteristic of the style Tango of your choice. There can be nothing sloppy about your dance posture if you want to be adequate as a social tango dancer.

Next there is the problem with the word rhythm. Some of you believe you have none! The reality is that any physical skill of a repetitive nature possesses the need for rhythm. Each of us demonstrates rhythm in our daily actions. The things we do physically are learned first by our muscles and then interpreted and recalled by our brains through the thought process. I will teach you to unlock the rhythm you already possess with the friendly use of your own voice. In this way we will learn to make friends with rhythm and use it coincidentally with the music.

Quickstart To Tango has been written with the KISS rule, that is "Keep it simple stupid." The charts in this book are easy to use and are followed by in-depth description. You will not have to be theoretically perfect to execute what is contained in the charts.
I have been teaching for over fifteen years and have come to understand that one key to successful learning is to use of all the senses. When a student applies all of his senses; of feeling, of

sight, and of hearing, to his dance education his recall becomes faster and more comprehensive. I will use analogies such as bicycle riding and ascending or descending a staircase to aid you in the feelings and controls necessary for dancing. Illustrations such as these are already familiar to your muscle memory. Therefore they will be easily applied to the tango.

Most of all, as you begin dance instruction you must abide by the following rule: always remember to treat yourself and your partner kindly, patiently, and forgivingly. Now it's time to get down to business!

What Is A Dance Step?

We will discuss what constitutes an actual dance step. The preliminary definition of a dance step is the body movement from one platform, known as a foot, to the next platform. This means you must move your body until you have achieved a new vertical position with all of your weight over the next foot. It is not enough to simply place your feet. You must complete the platforming of your body over the foot. Touching or tapping your foot will not teach your brain what is necessary to achieve a new point of comfortable balance.

Your brain is much happier if you learn to place or move your body to a designated location. In this way your legs and feet accommodate the movements of your body every single time. An example of this would be to pick up an object from one point in the room and place it at another point in the room. No thought is given about your legs or feet when doing this. I have had the opportunity over the years of my teaching to witness very intelligent and successful people stymied in their attempts to learn to dance. They have tried just learning choreographical patterns known as footsteps or figures without the understanding of a directional body weight change. The result of this "Touching the floor method," is frustrating because the student hasn't taught his brain to fully feel the body as an entity over the foot. For these reasons I have saved the actual choreography of Tango until the end of this text. You will be asked to develop the movement of Tango first by using the varied exercises I have prepared. They will teach you movement and control of your Tango.

3

In Quickstart To Tango whenever a command such as "left foot forward is given, please move your body as well as your left foot to a position in front of your right foot using a normal stride in the Tango style you are studying. One illustration that is quite understandable is to think of your feet as empty glasses and your body as a pitcher of water. You will complete a dance step in the same way you fill the class with water. The pitcher is lifted from one location and suspended over the glass. The water contained in the pitcher is freely and unrestrictedly poured into the class until the glass is filled. The water in the pitcher is not impeded in any way from being delivered to the base of the glass. Likewise, your body is lifted from one location toward another location and is delivered to that platform without impedance or restriction.

Your body is suspended over that location just long enough to load up the horizontal platform known as your foot. The location from which the body was lifted is known as your supporting or standing leg and foot. In the case of the pitcher your hand and arm supplied this lift. In the case of your body your legs and lower torso will supply the lift to move your body from the standing foot to the moving foot. Another example that you may relate to is the action of a rocket ship blasting off from a launching pad. The weight and pressure from the body's force propelled the body away from the dance floor and the supporting foot. Some of you know this to be Newton's third law of inertia plus the factors that relate to the acceleration of the mass of the body. The important thing to remember is a dance step is only complete when your body travels from one platform to the next. Those platforms are of course your feet.

"The Dynamic Duo"

Regardless of the dance or its inherent characteristics, each completed dance step must include what I call the "Dynamic Duo." The "Dynamic Duo," is comprised of two coincidental actions in two parts. The first segment of the, "Dynamic Duo," is what I refer to as **impact and correction**. The second segment of the "Dynamic Duo is referred to as **compression and leg swing**.

The following is a description of each segment. I firmly believe that as your dancing progresses the "Dynamic Duo" will aid you tremendously in achieving a higher level of dance ability.

Impact and Correction:

Impact occurs when the first supporting contact point of the foot meets the dance floor (Sometimes parts of the foot are used to contact the floor even though there is no desired weight change, i.e. outside edge of the foot).   Because impact is absorbed by the muscles located below the knees it is preferable to dance with very pliable ankles.   As described earlier the platforms known as the feet must fully accept the body's weight.   Positive impact cannot occur if the ankles repel the body's weight.   Simultaneously the body must correct its elevation and vertical position resulting from the forces of gravity and momentum.   Impact and correction are needed for every single dance step where a weight change occur.   The loss of elevation and vertical position occurs when the body is in flight or between the feet.   As the dancer improves his skill he will lose less elevation and vertical position by virtue of increased control of his muscularity.

This correction instantly brings the body to its desired elevation and vertical position for the next dance step.   Correction should happen virtually coincidentally with impact.   No matter how good the dancer gets, the natural forces of physics will affect each step.   Thus, upon foot impact, instantaneous correction of elevation and vertical position are vital.   Another measure of the dancer's ability will be how quickly he can correct his dance positions.   Loss of position is inherent, so taking and controlling a dance step becomes a process of continual correction!

Compression and Leg Swing

Compression is the event that occurs after correction.   By compression I mean the development of muscular power sufficient to propel the body to the next dance position.   Compression occurs by the muscular contraction of the portions of the leg above the knee through to the hip.   Compression also occurs when the dancer feels the spreading of the muscles and bones of his supporting foot.   This spreading action of the foot is due to the increased pressure caused by the body's weight plus the contraction of the muscles above the knee.   It is of the utmost importance for the dancer to feel the expansion of the foot on the dance floor so that he knows there is a stable and active platform from which to begin body flight.   It is often through this compression that the greatest feeling of musicality and rhythm is experienced by the dancer.   This compression will keep the dancer in character, movement, and music.   Without compression following impact, the dance movement becomes suspect, erratic, and stilted or static.   The growth of a dancer from the newcomer or beginner level can be measured by the frequency and depth of muscular compression throughout the leg and foot. I have always felt that a skill that a good teacher possesses is the ability to take a student from the visual and impact level of dance perception to the compressive and physical level of dance feeling.

The coincidence that occurs during the act of compression is the swing or positioning of the free leg and foot. The optimum time to swing the leg will always be the moment that the dancer's supporting foot feels the greatest compression and spreading within his dance shoe. This is your moment of greatest floor contact and connection. You will also notice that this becomes the point of greatest partner connection and contact. This therefore is a most important moment in your dancing and ability to create transition and retain musicality between your partner and yourself.

While moving into compression you have the greatest control to rotate, lead, position the free foot and leg. These all occur in the moment following impact and correction but before compression is complete. When compression is complete the body begins accelerating and traveling.

It is my sincere hope that my use and your understanding of the expression, "Dynamic duo," will assist your understanding of a dance step and how the sequence of the "Dynamic Duo" can improve your dance skills.

General technique for the new dancer

Learning Timing:

Our objective is to understand what we measure and to understand it as it applies to dance. Timing is more than hearing the bass register or drum beats in the music. Of course there are the drum beats or the steady pulse of one of the bass instruments such as a bass guitar that we must concern ourselves with to retain a steady cadence.

The ruler as an analogy, has increments, such as inches, defining equal segments. The beats of the percussion instruments define the equal increments of the music. We all know how to tap our feet. We do so in equal and steady pulses. The words, pulse and beat, come from that which is related to the heart — a heart beat.

Once in a while a new student will remark that he cannot hear the beats. He generally goes on to say that he is tone deaf. Generally the student has not learned to listen to the bass register of the music. He is searching for the beat in the lyrics of the song. The student feels, since he is not adept at singing or carrying a melody himself, that he must be tone deaf. The ability to carry a melody or being tone deaf has nothing to do with hearing the steady pulses made by the instruments used in the bass register of the music. If you feel this way about yourself consider knocking on a door. If you can hear the knocking, then you can certainly hear the beats in the music while you are learning to dance. Hearing the beats is something that you learn to listen for. Using the beats while learning to dance is the next topic of our discussion.

Each of the beats we hear has an identifiable time duration, or measurement, just as the illustration given of inches on a ruler. The issue we have to be most concerned with now is the allotment of time given to do a particular dance movement or step. A physical skill such as a dance step takes time to execute. Let's go back to the analogy of pouring water from a pitcher into a glass. Several physical events took place in a sequence. The pitcher had to be lifted from the table top and suspended over the orifice of the glass. Next, the contents of the pitcher had to be poured into the glass. These events could not have occurred all at the same time. What we must measure and allocate is the time expended to lift the body from the first platform and suspend the body in flight long enough to fill the next platform. The platform of which I speak are the supporting leg and foot.

This measured time is the beat structure or timing of the music to which you will be dancing. This beat structure or rhythm of the music will be counted in increments known as quick counts or slow counts. We must learn to be effective in our use of this quick and slow method of counting. Quick counts and slow counts will become part of your working dance vocabulary. These terms are commonly used by dancers and dance teachers to describe time.

The count in music known as a quick is equal to one increment of time. The count known as a slow is exactly twice the duration of a quick. In most cases throughout Quickstart To Tango, the count of a slow will equal one 2 beat increment of music. Therefore a slow count will be equal to two full beats of music. Once again I want to stress the duration of time a movement takes. In our practice exercises we will learn about our walking skills and further learn how they apply to the Tango. If the direction is given to take a walk to the count of a slow, we are saying that this Tango walk will take two beats or increments of music. Likewise, if the direction to move forward on a quick beat, then it will take one beat or increment of music to accomplish that forward step.

Again, by way of review, the Tango walk that is done to the musical count of a slow takes two beats of music. A walk to the musical count of a quick takes one beat of music. The duration of time in a quick movement can be thought of as a moment of compression of muscle and the subsequent release of the same muscle. This is exactly what your heart does. It draws blood in like a pump and distributes the blood on the release. The full cycle of your heart is measured as one heart beat or a quick. Walking on a slow count would be the equivalent of two full heart beats.

Another illustration that I like to use while teaching is that of a gardener or laborer shoveling dirt. One shovelful and its discharge is a quick. Two shovelfuls with their discharge would be a slow count. It will be much easier for you to count any Tango music with quicks and slows, and right now we want everything to be easy.

We will be counting aloud during our practice. It is hoped that counting aloud will become rhythmic as a cadence you hear when soldiers are marching. Hearing the rhythmic cadence of your voice counting slow, slow, slow, slow would be the equivalent of four of the basic walks taking a total of 8 beats of music.

Making The Music User Friendly!

Counting aloud during practice brings the familiar and friendly sound of your own voice into coincidence with the music. Hearing the music and your voice at the same time is a great device for getting right into the music rather than waiting to hear the music and then trying to begin. If you use the wait and begin method, by the time you hear the starting point you are already late.

Music has an unforgiving nature in that it is continuous and consistent. Internalizing the sound of the music in the same way we internalize the sound of our voice will give us the musical and rhythmic feeling. Overlapping this feeling with your hearing of the music will soon become automatic. At this point you will no longer need to count aloud. The only short cut to developing this skill is to compress the time by the frequent repetition of what I have suggested.

Your voice and the musical sound are energy. Foot pressure derived from your body weight on the dance floor is energy. When you put the two of these energy sources together, sound and foot pressure, they will quickly link the music to your balance and movement from one foot to the next. I cannot stress enough the importance of the previous statement! Why? Once again, dancing takes the use of full body weight over the foot to match the force found in the sound of music.

A Counting Pattern Just for Fun

I would like to illustrate a counting pattern just for beginners to have fun using. I want you to count the basic Tango pattern as follows: slow, slow, quick, quick, slow. We will learn more about the basic pattern in the American style of Tango as we go on in the book. For now I want you to count slow, slow, quick, quick, slow aloud so we can have fun with it. The sum total of that cadence of counting was equivalent to 8 beats or 8 increments of music. If we displayed them numerically we would have: one two, three four, five, six, seven eight. Please repeat this numbered pattern aloud with a pause where you read the comma. Once you become used to this verbalizing your cadence you will replace the numbers with the following letters: T, A, N, G, O.

The former is a way to remember basic timing in the American Tango. This alphabetical representation of the timing is measured in the following way.

The letter T replaces the first slow.

The letter A replaces the second slow.

The letter N replaces the first quick.

The letter G replaces the second quick.

The letter O replaces the final slow.

Once again, you will speak each letter rhythmically. You will always remember that the basic pattern in American style Tango will be counted T- A- N- G- O. This always brings a chuckle from the students but never seems to be forgotten.

The Movements Match The Musical Style

Each of the two dominant styles of Tango (American and Argentine) has its own characteristic in the music. I want to touch on several of these differences in this discussion of timing. This will help you to better understand each element of the dance figures in each style. The characteristic found in the music is what the tango dancer strives to insert in his dancing. After all, dancing is the personification of music.

American Tango Timing Characteristics

The American style of Tango uses a dominant, driving beat and staccato timing in its music. What staccato does to the music is shorten or delay the first moment of the beat or sound of the music. The musicians delay in starting the beat which accounts for the cat-like stalking movements of the dancers in the American style. Because each beat in a bar is accented, this staccato form of music is very powerful and masculine. Therefore, it is interpreted with very powerful but compact leg movements. The American style of Tango drives forward and then is danced to stop abruptly. The music used for the American style of Tango is measured in 2/4 timing. This means there are two beats to the bar making a Slow count one beat of music and a Quick 1/2 beat. The phrasing of this style of Tango is very specific and 8 bars are designated as a phrase. The speed at which tango is danced ranges between 30 and 33 bars of music per minute. The rhythm of this style of Tango is heard and felt through the bass register. This style of Tango music could be categorized as popular dance music in that the register timing, and tempo do not vary during the musical composition. The consistency of the American Tango music is matched by the consistency of the American style dance figures. When dancing the American style of Tango, virtually all figure patterns will retain the same timing for each and every usage of **that** figure, especially at the basic level. A ballroom dancer will interpret the music with the variety of figure patterns and their flight across the dance floor.

Argentine Tango Timing Characteristics

By contrast the Argentine Tango music is a leggiero (connected, smoother, & lighter) type of music. Its properties are more akin to or inherent in Latin American music particularly the Bolero Rumba (also very smooth without staccato). The physical usage of the legs and feet are similar to the Bolero. We do not drive with our legs nor do we take our feet off the floor in progressive movements. The balls of the feet which carry the weight in Argentine Tango skim the dance floor.

The time intervals between dance movements, figure patterns, and figure types are actually more whimsical. Many factors control or even dictate the speed at which figure types are danced in Argentine Tango. In this case we may take the word whimsy to be synonymous with the idea of dance improvisation. The speed of the dance patterns can change contingent on the timing or register changes one finds in Argentine Tango music. Quick and slow beats may vary in their time duration through the course of the same music. As in jazz or classical music the registers do change and are even described as movements themselves.

The comfort and experience of the Argentine Tango dancer can also dictate the speed at which the figures are interpreted. One very unusual characteristic of the Argentine style music is that the musicians presenting the musical composition can actually perform together in different time registers. Because of this, the dancer may interpret the mood, melody, or even the lyrics to better personify this form of Tango. While this may seem confusing to the dancer, he actually has the luxury of interpreting the dance movements and their speed. One well known characteristic is, if their is improvisation it is conveyed through the leader as the follower develops the mentality of a slow rhythm step as opposed to a quick rhythm. This makes the leading and following of the Argentine Tango very much like the American Foxtrot where the follower also anticipates the slow rhythm. In both dances the follower must be made to feel the quick movement.

The Argentine Tango dancer actually can portray an emotional story in his dancing. Like the music, we tell a story to each other through our varied movements and figure types. The speed or even the lack of movement helps us to convey our feelings and intentions to our partner. As with jazz music, the dancer can show off his skills by playing riffs and trilling in the same way a saxophone or trumpet player does. A jazz solo will often have a timing register different and apart from the main musical composition. When the solo is completed the instrument will blend back into the phrasing of the music. The dancer in like kind will blend his dancing back into the music after having mirrored the instrumental portion of the music he is interpreting. There are many musical compositions used in Argentine Tango in which the phrasing is very defined and easily heard and felt. When the music allows for a stricter tempo the Argentine dancer will use what is called cadencia. Cadencia is interpreting your choreography so that your beginning and finish of a series of patterns will conclude simultaneously with the completion of eight bars of music. Cadencia in English simply means phrasing. It is really only important to the performance level of Tango when you are dancing to a specific musical composition over and over without improvisation. At the social level of Argentine Tango the execution of cadencia in a strict sense is less important and it is conceivable that you will never have to be concerned with it.

Let us briefly summarize what we have learned about timing in tango:

1. Each foot step or dance step you will take will require a timed body weight change to be recognized as a successfully completed dance step.

2. A Tango movement counted as a slow will take two beats or increments of music. A Tango movement that will take one beat of music known as a quick.
The leg, foot, and body movement must all coincide within the designated time period the particular dance step calls for or allows.

3. You must learn to listen specifically to the base line of the music to hear the cadence of the drum or other percussion beats.

4. Counting aloud will familiarize you with the beat and facilitate your learning

5. You have learned to verbalize the alphabetic rhythmic count of T-A-N-G-O as a practice exercise.

6. You will become aware that there are many differences between American Tango and Argentine Tango.

Recommended List of CD's:

The Argentine Style:

1-Fransisco Canaro, La Melodia de Nuestros Adios, El Bandoneon, Catalog # AEB 030   Slow but swinging tangos, milongas, and waltzes- great for practice and play.

2- Carlos DiSarli, Instrumental, DBN/BMG Argentina, Catalog # ADBG 297   The slow steady walking beat used by good teachers like Juan Bruno.

3- Juan D'Arienzo, La Cumparsita(1935-39), El Bandoneon, #AEB 084

The "King of the Beat".   Music for sophisticated and fast salon vocabulary.

4- Osvaldo Pugliese, From Argentina to the World, EMI Argentina, # ADEM 857   The inspiration for new tango. These are the dramatic and emotional tangos popular among stage performers yet also played for social dancing.

5- Anibal Troilo, El Immortal Pichuco (1941), El Bandoneon, #AEB 001

The mythological bandoneon player who defines the instrument. The few instrumental recordings from the forties (There are three on this disc.) are played at every social dance in Buenos Aires.

6- Cacho Tirao, Forever Music, # AFM 9713

Tangos on virtuoso solo guitar for listening and dreaming.

7- Forever Tango, by the Company, # FT 001

The sound track from the great Broadway show of 1997-8.

You may obtain a free catalog for the list to the right from:
Bridge To The Tango Catalog
B-2 Juniper East
Yarmouth, ME 04096
Toll free:
(888) DTango7 (382-6467)

You may obtain a free catalog for the list to the right from:
Dance Vision, International
8933 W. Sahara Ave.
Suite 101
Las Vegas, Nevada
        89117-5826
Tel: (1) 800-851-2813
E-mail:
Info@dancevision.com

The American Style Tango:

1.James Last, Tango, 1981 Polydor International

The entire CD is excellent and one of my favorites and available at your local music store.

2.Percy Faith, Sombras from 1 of several good Tangos from the Casa Musica Collections

12

Movement and Control for Tango
The "Quickstart Exercises":

Learning Its Development with Practice Exercises

This section will provide lots of fun while preparing you to dance Tango together. This section of Quickstart To Tango may be the most important part of this book for you.   We will cover some basic Tango movements and body positions.   I want to give you some exercises that will help you achieve the atmosphere and characteristics of the Tango. Before beginning the Tango exercises select your favorite Tango music as it will provide inspiration and rhythm.

Note of caution:

Before you attempt any of the following exercises, movements, or procedure consider your present physical condition.   If you have any physical pain prior to dancing or exercising for dance, please consult your physician before beginning.   **If you normally need to use a hand rail when traveling a staircase, do not do the staircase procedure.**   You do not need to follow the staircase illustration to learn the Tango.   This exercise is to help you evaluate your ribcage control.   Again it is only an illustration and not a prerequisite for dancing Tango.

The Staircase Scenario—The Ribcage

I have stressed the importance of ribcage and abdominal control. Here is one of the best procedures I know of to help you evaluate these controls.   We are going to ascend and descend a staircase. The   purpose of this staircase illustration is to tie together the physical control and mental concentration.   As you rehearse these exercises, learn the Tango choreography, and move with Tango characteristic, you are developing inherent qualities of a tango dancer.   You might say you are developing Tango instincts.   These Tango instincts and partnering instincts in general are required to dance Tango.

There is jeopardy inherent in traveling a staircase, particularly if you are not using a handrail.   You learned this long ago.   At this time I want you to travel up and down a staircase several times without the use of a handrail (Please note my earlier caution -- thank you).   Your brain and body move to an automatic control and search for balance. The brain focuses these controls in the abdominal region and ribcage. Although falling down a staircase has a much greater potential for injury than falling down during a dance, I want you to sense the same jeopardy. Falling out of balance, by losing control of your abdominal area and ribcage, while dancing with a partner is hazardous to your danceability. Beware; the dance police will arrest you for loss of control. Because music is continuous, it is unforgiving in the same way that gravity is. Loss of balance on the staircase, like loss of balance on the dance floor is the loss of vertical control. The beginning of loss of balance while dancing is related to the ribcage. When loss of balance occurs your survival instincts are activated and your brain tries to bring your movement to a halt. This therefore will put you out of the music or off timing. For most people, their structuring of the body while ascending or descending a staircase is superior to their usual body position. You and your partner must instinctively control your bodies at least as well as you control them on the staircase.

If body control is second nature on a staircase, then it can become second nature on the dance floor with your partner. We must bring balance to the dance partnership rather than searching for it from our partner as we might search for a handrail along the staircase. Basically we want to create a dance couple that is one unit, not two individuals. Your torso, your arms, and your head are supported from below. You must use your legs for this work and not your partner's.

Throughout your Tango dancing, think of your ribcage as one railroad track. The second rail of these tracks will be a line parallel with the floor and passing through your hip bones. This advice will serve you well. You must not let the train jump the tracks! Your ribcage must experience lift on each and every dance step. An experienced dancer will flex each and every muscle surrounding and immediately below the ribcage. This muscular flex includes both front and back of the ribcage. I cannot stress enough the importance of making this a good habit from the beginning of your dance experience!

You may want to try ascending and descending the staircase to music. Use both slow counts and quick counts. Be very deliberate and conscious of your balance in both the positive lift and negative lowering on each stair tread. This little exercise can help make you aware of the combined usage of the knee and ankle along with the muscles they impact. These are both factors in each dance step.

Learning Leg Swing with Body Control— A comprehensive exercise

To dance successfully with a partner proper leg swing becomes a necessity. Leg swing must never affect the body's balance, nor should it create inadvertent movement. Beginners should be aware of leg swing skills. People dance for years without being aware of this factor and its impact on their dancing. Our concern is to remain upright and in control of the upright position while dancing. Leg swings will either complement or become a detriment to your dancing or attempt at dancing. Heavy or forceful swing of the legs will jerk the body out of its good position and will necessitate holding on to your partner as if he were a handrail. We will learn an exercise that will give you the mental and physical idea of leg swings while dancing the Tango.

The following is an exercise best done with your partner although it can be done alone and with Tango music for motivation! This exercise is probably the most comprehensive leg building and leg swing exercise a dance couple can do together. I would include it in a warm up prior to a practice session.

Practice Position for Leg Swing

I want you and your partner to join arms. Your hands will lightly clasp the area of your partner's elbows. This would be similar to surrounding hula-hoop with your arms and the arms of your partner. You will brace your knees (that is limiting the bend of the knee to where flex and firming of the hamstring is felt and not beyond that point) and stand in opposition as you will approximate the position of the Tango. The difference is your feet may be 10 to 15 inches away from your partner's feet. In this exercise you will pulse at the knees without losing the bracing effect. Rhythmic pulsing will virtually eliminate rise while you are dancing the Tango. This is important because there is no rise and fall or changes in overall elevation in the American style of the Tango. In the Argentine style of the Tango the ability to control rise is imperative during progressive movement. You would never want a bouncing action in the Argentine Tango. With every slow count of the music (two beats of music) you and your partner will swing your opposing legs (his left to her right) with a full pendulum action of the thighs. Although the thigh portion of the leg will achieve a full pendulum swing, the area from the knee down to the foot will never fully straighten. The lower leg will almost straighten. By contrast, the ballroom swing of the leg in such dances as the Foxtrot and Waltz exercise would fully straighten. Straightening is not to be confused with locking the knee. The action of thigh swing without the full straightening of the lower leg will mimic precisely what occurs during a Tango walk. Using the same slow rhythm, a pulsing up through the thigh and a coincidental contraction of the abdominal wall occur when releasing the foot from

Practice Position for Leg Swing

15

the floor. A pulsing down through the knee of the supporting leg will occur when placing the foot down to the floor or at the end of the swing. The foot will skim ever so slightly in the line of the pendulum swing. In the American Tango the foot may be released from the floor. By contrast, in the Argentine Tango the foot should never leave the floor but skim smoothly in line with the pendulum. When the muscles fatigue, just switch the exercise to the alternate leg by moving either forward or backward with a suitable Tango walk. Make sure you do these walks in rhythm. It is not necessary to restrict yourselves to just one walk at a time. As long as you do an odd number of walking steps you will have switched legs.

The overall goal of the preceding exercise is to swing the leg fully as described and not experience any inadvertent movement of your or your partner's body. You will achieve greater leg speed without affecting either of your balances. Your legs will build stamina and strength from this simple exercise. This is good because the greater the inherent strength of the leg the less the feeling of exertion. Thus, a softer and faster leg action will result from having stronger legs. You will have to exert abdominal control to swing the leg with complete isolation. This therefore will improve your abdominal strength. You will quickly feel the sequence of muscular events necessary to do a Tango walk forward or backward with the music. The pulsing action of the knees, wrists, and elbows will produce connection through the frame of the couple. Connection is a positive or forward resistance to your partner with finesse. I use the word finesse to indicate that resistance should be kept as light as possible. Use only the resistance necessary to complete and sustain the connection.

Continued practice of this exercise, particularly with your partner, will improve your overall body flight. You should also take great pride in the fact that you no longer need your partner to sustain your own balance. You should strive to reach the time when you can perform this exercise in virtual body contact with your partner as you would dance Tango with them.

The Tango Solo Stalking Walks Exercise:

An exercise for the development of The Inherent Curving Tango walking movements - Forward and Backward .

Here is an exercise that is pure "Fun, fun, fun," but do not lose sight of the fact that you will learn much about Tango walks forward and backward. This exercise will be useful for **both** styles of Tango. I will endeavor to describe the differences.

Tango stalking walks are fun to do with as many people as possible. I have used this procedure in group classes of 15 to 20 people. Smiles are on the faces of all while the Tango music is playing. This movement exercise is fine to do by yourself, however. It is very effective with you and your partner. All you need is some space and an object like a stool at the center of that space. As an added incentive place a red rose on the object in the center of the circle. Select your favorite Tango music. It will serve as wonderful inspiration while at the same time providing motivation. Actors present a role by acting "in character." Tango must also be danced in character.

A note to the reader: By their nature, Tango walks tend to curve. It may be wise for the beginner to develop a good standard of forward and backward walking with a partner. The book Quickstart To Social Dancing contains developmental walking exercises for the beginner in any general partner dancing. It may be wise to gain an appreciation of good movements forward and backward in a straight line before a clear physical understanding is gained in curving movements forward and backward.

As you perform the following exercise work on each element individually and then piggyback the next element with your former development. This exercise can be more fun than two people are supposed to have in a vertical position. Therefore, repeat the circle several times before you add more of the elements found in the Tango characteristics. Include with each level of the stalking walks, verbal counts without music and then with music. This will develop comprehensive muscle memory in your Tango.

The Starting Point

The exercise: Align yourself with your partner, and begin to move casually in opposition to each other. Begin to feel the idea of curving movements while keeping your eye on your partner. This becomes the first phase of your exercise.

Gaining Understanding: I want to discuss this exercise with the use of two people. You will be circling the object in the center of the dance floor. One dancer will stand at 12 o'clock and the other at six o'clock. Your initial rotation will commence counter clockwise as this will be the natural direction of Tango. The gentleman will begin this walking exercise facing the circumference of the circle and moving counter clockwise. The lady will move back around the circumference of the circle moving counter clockwise.

Move in even and opposite increments keeping six increments of the clock between you (example 1 o'clock to 7 o'clock). Greater appreciation of your partner and that of the Tango itself will be achieved if these stalking walks are felt by each partner both forward and backward as well as clockwise and counter clockwise. **You will want to practice leading each other.** This will most assuredly aid in your discovery and development of Tango's leading and following. You will gain physical and spatial appreciation of what your partner requires you to do to move comfortably with each other. Brute strength should never be the answer.

As dancers we will always finesse our strength so it is applied vertically to the dance floor rather than to our partner! Remember, in dancing there are three progressive movements: forward, backwards, and sideways. Any of the three can move right or left by curving, turning, or stepping to the side. These forward, side or backward movements can be done in line with your partner (normal dance position), outside partner (the man slightly more to the left of his partner), partner outside (the man slightly to the right of his partner). Additionally they can be accomplished with either foot. You will want to practice all of these walking variations. In Tango, a single walking movement is construed to be a full figure!

The Mental Attitude Becomes The Physical Approach for Partnering in Progressive Movement:

Each movement in dance must have a specific purpose. Whether the movement is made by the entirety of the body, or by any singular extremity, there must be a purpose. To this end, the individual must be committed both aesthetically and emotionally as well as physically. This commitment can become the yardstick by which we can measure our personal growth in dancing.

The specific purpose of any movement must be taken very seriously if we are dancing as a couple. The leader's movement across the dance floor creates the follower's movement. The follower will develop the movement spatially and then give it back to the leader to redevelop. The leader's body follows the partner's body once the transaction of lead has been indicated. This may sound like a nuance to many of you. Nevertheless, it is a fact. Simply stated, when the follower begins to travel she opens a door for the leader to enter. It is like an empty room which you wish to furnish. You must cross the threshold and enter carrying any objects that are suitable for the design of that room. The dance figure is the room; and your body, its shaping, length, and extremity usage are the objects you place there. The leader must remain cognizant at all times of the space he must fill with his body. The leader must do this quickly and completely. There is no time to stop dancing and admire your work. Your finish of any single step is the beginning of the next movement or figure. The leader must finish well, to once again, take the lead. Good leading comes only from good finishing.

The man and the lady need enough room within the couple's frame on every dance figure, while at the same time, being careful not to make movements so as to avoid each other. Such avoidance would change the directional tangents unnecessarily and undesirably. Reciprocity of body angles allows for comfortable passage of the bodies. Think of a revolving door as an analogy. It is the responsibility of each partner to retain a solid geometric line of energy directed both through the feet vertically and across the dance floor laterally. Regardless, of which member of the couple is traveling backward, the space they provide by doing so is a form of invitation. That invitation must say come through to the point where we are to meet again. This invitation is accepted willingly and aggressively.

This will provide the feeling of togetherness and oneness. The physical acceptance of the invitation is the movement through the partner's former position.
Now, you have created the good look!

Elevation of The Head and Body

The exercise: Once you have begun circling with your partner, become conscious of a line parallel to the floor, at approximately your eye level. As you continue to circle with the stalking walks attempt to remain at the same elevation. This will help you to understand the intentional omission of rise and fall in your development of Tango. Make sure that you observe the dynamic duo on each completed dance step during the entire exercise. (We discussed this dynamic duo in the section titled What Is A Dance Step? As a reminder they are **impact and correction -- then -- compression and leg swing.**)

Gaining Understanding: Each dancer participating in this movement exercise will stalk the object in the center of the circle as well as the dancer on the opposing line. This is important because you must look where you are going on the dance floor. This may sound remedial, but nothing positive happens when the dancer does not focus where he is going or becomes introspective. Looking at your feet is deadly to your balance and muscle memory while trying to learn either style of Tango. It is considered bad dance form!

The Argentine Style of Tango allows for the lady to have a downcast appearance, but in no way is she allowed to drop her head out of the control of her neck and frame. Never confuse the turned position of the lady's head coupled with the downcast appearance as a loss of head or upper body control. Argentine Tango dancers do not look at their own feet. They look at the footwork of others for artistic motivation and inspiration. This creates the atmosphere of improvisation!

No matter what type of Tango the couple chooses to develop, for good dancing the balance of the head must be considered. The elevation at which the body and head travel throughout this stalking exercise remains absolutely the same. When a dance couple travel at one consistent elevation we say they have no rise and fall. In either style most steps that involve progressive movement have no rise and fall. These traveling figures are danced with a pre-flexed or bracing action through the knees and upon contact the supporting knee is squeezed by a controlled flex within the upper-thigh. The dancer can prevent rise and fall by using his eyes to sustain a level of elevation. To do this focus on one consistent elevation around the exterior of the room. Focus at eye level or slightly above for the American style or slightly below for Argentine. It is important in both styles of Tango to negate, deter, or inhibit rise and fall. Its use is reserved for stationary or stationary rotating figures. In this way the partners will read each other's movements correctly.

There is no rise and fall in the basic walking movements in either American or Argentine Tango

Argentine Tango dancers position their heads for inspiration!

Argentine Tango Dance Position

Beginning To Move, "In Time"

The exercise: The body of each dancer must proceed (forward-man, backward-lady) on the designated circumference taking the same length of stride on each step. We will use slow walks (two beats of music per walk) to begin the movement of Tango walking. Initially begin this movement exercise without music. In place of the music each dancer participating should count aloud as follows: one, two; three, four; five, six; seven, eight; for a total of 4 Tango walks. Introduce the music and continue to count aloud. In this way you will feel a part of the music or, "In the music." Once you have gained control of the rhythm and movement with music, you may vary the counting pattern to include quick counts of music. Earlier in this text we discussed timing. At that time I gave you the example of spelling Tango as a musical timing device (See: Timing in Tango). Please spell aloud T-A-N-G-O for a total of 8 musical counts. Have some fun with your practice partner. Alphabetize your Tango counts and add this to your stalking walks with some good Tango music.

American Tango Dance Position

Gaining Understanding: For the beginner counting aloud is quite important. The new dancer often feels attacked by the music rather than feeling part of it. The friendly sound of your voice will integrate the music with your muscular response, and in this way the music becomes user friendly. You may have already learned that you are actually counting the flight of your body between each platform known as your feet and also the periods of time your body passes from the entry point of your foot to the exit point of your foot. As you become a better dancer you will spend more and more time on your foot rather than between your feet. Simply stated the longer you can remain on your foot the better control, balance, and musicality you can create.

Helpful hint: I am very sure by now that you realize the importance of controlling your body while moving with a partner. The human body does not move well if stability is not achieved. A good idea is to imagine your spinal column passing through the front of your ribcage as you begin to move forward. By contrast, please feel your abdominal wall moving toward your spinal column as you begin to move backward. Be sure to keep the vertical alignments of your shoulders, ribs, and hips intact. This will help!

How to Negotiate The Circle

The accuracy of this circular exercise has particular bearing on the American style where we stress a curving walk.

The Argentine walk or stroll curves according to the design of the leader

American Style Heel Lead

The exercise: You should now be able to add timing and balance without rise and fall to your curving walks. If you have the room to do so attempt to develop a circle based on eight sets of curving walks. When approximately eight sets, 16 steps, of curving walks complete a full circle, you have discovered the normal curve for a tango basic. To fully gain appreciation of this exercise I want you visualize an imaginary circle around the dance floor you are in. With your imaginary circle in place, each left foot forward will find the left side of that foot placed just on the outside of the imaginary line. When the right foot moves forward the left side of the right foot will contact the imaginary circumference line.

Gentlemen, when you stride forward with your right side it will be felt as more of a release from some of the torque a left foot forward walk in CBMP. The right side of the body will remain advanced slightly forward of the left side of the body. The right shoulder, ribcage, and hip aligned and moving together are known as a **right shoulder lead**. This will keep the right body side of the gentleman slightly ahead of his left body side.

Ladies, once again the opposite is true for your Tango. Your left side will advance slightly ahead of your right side on all of your left walks backwards. Therefore you have a left shoulder leading on a left backward walk. The crossing actions of the legs particularly in the Argentine style and the promenade movements of the American style will be greatly assisted by what happens on the follower's left side. Control of this body torque increases sensitivity in the language of lead and follows.

Gaining Understanding: This type of left foot placement will be known as CBMP (Contra-Body Movement Position of the Foot). CBMP occurs when the moving foot crosses the plane of the standing foot without the body turning. CBMP occurs when the left side of the left foot is placed outside the circumference of our imaginary circle. CBMP produces a streamlining effect when the partners stand in a frame called, "Outside partner or partner outside." We will demonstrate these positions later in the text. This walking will produce the precedent for CBM and CBMP.

Using Good Foot Contact

Argentine Style Tango:

The initial contact with the floor for the dancer will be the appropriate edge of the foot and then the ball of the foot. The ball of the foot carries the weight in the Argentine style. We must learn to use the sensitivity and strength of the edges of the big toe, first, to create and maintain good floor contact and pressure. Using your big toe can be thought of as making a fist with your foot. This will keep good tone throughout your leg and help you to create leg and foot line. Keeping the idea of a fist will help you to implement this technique when dancing. You will find the big toe is a great friend to your dancing, in general, and Argentine Tango specifically, if you have never tried using it before. When you enter your foot with firmness felt in the big toe your ability to achieve balance and smoothness is greatly enhanced. If you are familiar with the slower Latin dances like the Bolero Rumba you are somewhat familiar with this foot action and pressure. This characterization in foot usage is very sleek and smooth, almost creamy, in progressive movement.

Argentine Walk with the collection of the free foot

Also of major importance to this style will be the collection of the feet in the midst of striding. This means as the weight is taken onto the moving foot and the alternate foot is allowed to skim, toned to the dance floor, to a position under the corresponding hip. Ballroom Tango dancers new to the Argentine style can think of this action of the "Stroll," as a Tango draw that moves either forward or backward. Traveling backwards will involve a skimming toe and the ball of the foot. In This style of Tango it is permissible to peer around to the rear when you are negotiating a backward Tango walk.

The Crossed Feet Strolling Exercise:

I want to prepare you early in this text for the culture shock of Crossed Feet, particularly, if you are new to dancing! Crossed Feet occur when both partner's are changing weight to the same foot in harmony. In general ballroom dancing this is known as using the same foot. The use of Crossed Feet is essential to develop an authentic social style of Argentine Tango.

Argentine Style crossed feet Both using right foot

I do not want to perplex you at this time so we will make this exercise very simple. Take the practice position from the leg swing exercise and begin to travel in your practice space or around your circle. Both partners will use the same feet at the same time moving both forward and backward. Count these walks with a slow rhythm using the footwork previously described. You may attempt to travel towards the left and right side of your partner in both directions.

Make sure you take turns leading so there is a smooth rhythmic physical exchange with each other. Later in this text we will develop and use of Crossed Feet positions.

American Style Walk and Footwork

American Style Tango:

The initial **pressure** of the left foot is felt on the outside or left side of that foot. The initial **pressure** of the right foot is found on the inside or left side of the right foot. The initial pressure in the foot is then dispersed throughout the whole foot. Try to develop as many contact points as possible when dancing. Visualize your spinal column in perpendicular alignment, traveling incrementally and vertically through these contact points in any direction. I highly recommend that when dancing feel your feet against the dance floor as if you where not wearing shoes. This will help you to achieve stability in your walking movements. One example of foot entry would be when the man takes the left foot forward he feels initial contact on the left side of his foot.

In addition to the edges of the foot please note that the initial **contact** with the dance floor for the partner going forward will be the heel, and the initial contact going backwards will be the ball of the foot. The feet are allowed to delay and then slightly release from the floor creating a very sharp, crisp movement. This enhances the characterization of the staccato music in progressive movement. The length of stride in the American style of Tango is different than in other progressive ballroom dances. It would be considered a medium stride by comparison to a Foxtrot or Waltz.

Developing Center Feeling and Control:

As we have spoken of earlier, while the placement your feet or swinging your thighs takes place the tango dancer must feel compression and torque through the abdominal area. This is a good time to experience the very slight twist to the left of the ribcage without the hip and pelvis moving. This twist was also spoken about in the development of the Tango frame. It is created, felt, and held through the center of the back as well as the abdominal wall. Once the relationship between ribcage, shoulders, and pelvis has been established it remains relatively static. When placing the feet in contact with the dance floor, compression both in the abdominal wall and in the thigh muscles bracing against the knees must be felt. Additionally you must not release either foot from the floor until you feel clear contact and weighted pressure.

American Style Man's Right Foot Walk

Individual Body Positions for Men and Women:

For the man the greatest compression will be felt as you stride forward with the left leg. The placement of the left foot as described above should always produce the following result. The right hip, the right side of the ribcage, as well as the right shoulder advancing slightly forward of the comparable body parts on the left side. These three remain vertically aligned with each other through the course of your Tango walking exercise. When the tango dancer is taking the left foot forward, say either to yourself or aloud "compress." This type of movement is known as CBM. The definition of CBM: is rotating the opposing hip and shoulder together with the ribcage, toward the direction of the moving leg. CBM is used in greater or lesser degrees to begin virtually every turning dance progression or movement. What is more important is you have created and are utilizing CBM. The gentleman will use CBM on every step forward with the left foot in Tango.

CBM exists for the woman as well and is an intricate part of her Tango experience. Ladies should and will experience CBM on every backward right leg walks in the Tango. Additionally this means you will feel the left side of your body advancing slightly before the right side of your body when moving in CBM. This, of course, accommodates the movement of the gentleman. The usage of CBM is vital to both styles of Tango. The rotations including "Ochos" in the Argentine and "Fans" in the American Tangos require intensification of CBM. Additionally the sharpness of head actions in the American style of Tango is assisted by the use of CBM. Please observe that when initiating CBM, it must begin from your standing leg and not your waist. It may be easier to feel the development of CBM by using the hips and thigh first and allowing the torque you have already developed in your Tango position to bring the shoulder and ribcage into the proper alignment. Always remember that the use of CBM will streamline the couple and assist the couple in and out of positions of outside partner. "Moving To The Cross" a specific pattern in Argentine Tango, will also be greatly assisted by initiating CBM!

CBM, Leg Veer, and CBMP are indeed General Ballroom descriptions. These descriptions have been adopted in many forms of partner dancing and I feel offer a very concise method of describing these common positions. I hope that if these terms are new, you will also find them useful.

Walking in CBM and CBMP are indicative of the Ballroom Tango. Using these two devices are wonderful for any portion of rotation and concluding leg lines in either style of Tango!

25

Leg Action and Its Feeling For Men and Women

Now that you have begun your movements in these exercises, there are some advanced feelings and positions you should develop and monitor. Monitoring muscle contraction and expansion as we have discussed is a very important part of your dance development. Students often complain that there is too much to remember. Muscle memory and muscle monitoring will make your intellectual appraisal of dancing much easier. All you will have to remember is where you are going. When your muscles move out of sequence or your body moves out of alignment, the proverbial bell will go off in your head and you will feel where you need correction.

The first new position I want you to develop is called leg veer. A secondary result of leg veer is knee veer and its compression. Leg veer can be described as a feeling of compression in which the thighs and knees of the dancer slightly compress towards each other while the dancer's body is directly over the final contact point his foot. Leg veer gives the dancer a feeling of strength enabling greater control. I often instruct new Tango and Swing dancers to develop leg veer by rolling up a towel or placing a small throw pillow between their upper thighs very close if not in contact with their crotch. Moving in promenade, sideways, or in small steps forward or backward, with the towel between the thighs will exhibit to the dancer greater strength, balance, and control. Many experts feel that without leg veer there is a missing link in the character of Tango. This is particularly true in the American style of Tango. Argentine Tango essentially danced on the balls of the feet, will benefit greatly by leg veer. The closing action of "el Resolucion" to the balls of both feet will be done perfectly with this technique. It will keep the toes pointing slightly at each other and the feet just apart. Another important application of leg veer will be in the elimination of rise and fall. Later on in the choreographical patterns of Tango we will discuss the closing actions of the leg, when drawn together leg veer will be in applied to your physical technique. To test leg veer dance for a few moments with the knees turned out from your center, then pointed absolutely forward, and then with leg veer. You decide!

The exercise: Once you have built all the elements discussed above into these exercises, do them a dozen or more times by yourself. This means without contact with a partner. You are now more than ready to begin the choreography of Tango.

Gaining Understanding: The actions of compression and release will begin to teach you to characterize the Tango. These feelings will create a rhythm for you and assist your muscle memory in developing your Tango movements.

26

Rotation in Tango

Introduction to Rotation

I now want to discuss rotation as it is used in Tango. The most popular forms of rotation found in Tango would be the Fans in the Ballroom style and the various Ochos in the Argentine style. Both of these figures are initiated by one of the partners and concentrate heavily around the established center of rotation of their partner. There are also many dance figures in each style that include a pivoting action by the couple itself, as well as additional forms of coincidental rotation or curve by both partners. All of these will be clarified in the following paragraphs. We will concentrate our discussion of rotation mainly around the concept of leading and following. You will however find this portion of the text very useful in personal rotation and spins in dancing. I will attempt to give you some easy to use illustrations and tips of technique to improve the quality of your Tango dancing and your general partner dancing as well. At the end of this discussion, you will also find a description of holding the foot in CBMP. This is a very useful and aesthetically pleasing position for the foot and leg. It is used in both styles of Tango. Holding the foot in CBMP accents their partner's rotation.

Definition of Body Torque:

A twisting effort initiated by the muscles of the body, predominantly around the ribcage and abdominal wall, which when applied to the various lateral assemblies causes the body to turn about it axis of rotation. The time to best experience and utilize body torque is after the impact and correction, and just as compression ensues, as described as part of the, "Dynamic Duo" (See: Understanding A Dance Step). This axis of rotation can be thought of as an imaginary laser beam passing through the skull, the entirety of the spinal column, and continuing through the standing or supporting leg, to the focal contact point of the foot on the floor. In the vast majority of cases this contact point will be the ball of the foot.

To best illustrate the action of body torque, I want you to fold a bath towel to approximately 3 feet in length and begin twisting each end of the towel until it becomes quite firm. The center of the towel can be likened to the main part of your torso. Release the towel by holding either the bottom or the top of the twisted portion, your choice, and you will see the remainder of the towel explode into rotation. You have now seen how a soft inanimate object can produce powerful torque and rotation. Now let's liken this to your dancing. Simply, concentrate your energies on your center rather than on your extremities (hands, legs & feet, shoulders) and you will see rotation flourish in your dancing.

The Rule of Body Torque:

When the Leader is forward or moving forward on his left foot he will create the torque for left or counter clockwise rotation. Once the establishment of the new vertical axis has been created over his left foot, the dancer can either rotate or lead the counter clockwise rotation. The exact opposite is true when moving towards his right foot and leg. In this case the rotation will be right or clockwise. The rule continues with backward movements and dance steps. The right foot back produces left torque and left foot back produces right torque in the dancer's body. With respect to his partner the reciprocal is true, therefore the couple's connected dance frame works harmoniously with the Rule of Body Torque.

Once you have experimented with, as well as physically and mentally digested this rule of torque, you will become a better dancer. Remember always step in a manner to create the new vertical axis and then use the torque for rotation in leading or following. Torque and its development through the abdominal area is also described in your Tango exercises.

The Rule of "Step, Then Turn" :

Once a dance step has commenced with the objective of rotation or leading rotation the rule of "Step, Then Turn," must be applied. This technique is very simple to understand. However it requires good form throughout your dancing. We have already discussed what a good dance step consists of. The first portion of the "Step, Then Turn," rule is take a technically good dance step!

In the case of leading and following, the follower must achieve a position of a new vertical axis on which to rotate before the rotation should be led or even attempted. The optimum time for this to occur is just as the dancer's knees are passing each other. At this moment the body is centered perfectly. When we stand normally our knees are together and all the weight of our body is in line vertically. When moving, the body turns best when all, or the great majority, of our weight including our legs is in line vertically. Achieving a position of, in line vertically, is then the key to the "Step, Then Turn" rule. When you begin to apply both of the above rules

Ballroom Fan after the lady has created a good vertical axis on her right foot

28

you will find that making up to one half a rotation in your dancing will become effortless.

Leading and following in either style of Tango is never about power or strength. Brute force is always a negative should the need arrive to empower your power either to progressive movement or rotation. Physical habits and concentration (both mentally and physically) that create good balance & frame. Neat placement and release of the feet in dancing will result in good balance. Arbitrary release of the feet from the dance floor is a great cause for problems in leading and following a dance pattern. Sloppy use of the feet will often let your frame move beyond the targeted area into a position that must be counter-balanced by your partner. This would be a violation of what I describe as the, "Never, Never Rule." NEVER move in such a way as to negatively affect your partner's balance. This definitely includes the use of hands and arms while leading or following. Yanking, pushing, or pulling have nothing whatever to do with the Tango. Internalize your strength rather than letting it flow out of your extremities!

I know that record turntables are becoming scarce, but here is a helpful illustration for leading. Place your middle finger right next to the spindle at the center of the turntable. Attempt to rotate the turntable and you will find there is a good amount of resistance. Now move the same finger to the outside edge of the turntable and attempt to rotate it. If you anticipated and applied the same force, I bet it spun right out of your control. The effort to turn it is many time less than at the center. The further we move from the center, the force required is required. What we learn here is that with a good vertical center (spindle) the outer circumference a balanced object will rotate with great ease.

The application of this knowledge to our Tango will work something like this: Create a wide dance frame with the upper arms away from the ribcage, and control your vertical center. Notice that the periphery of the body become responsive to the lightest pressure from your partner. Therefore, it will only be a matter of speed and timing to generate a change of direction or spot rotation. A breeze is enough pressure to turn your partner or to turn with your partner. Reserve your strength to create your own vertical elevation and internal muscular control! Use this rather than extremity force and challenging the partner's balance and center. If you need to generate greater amounts of rotation or sharpness in rotation do so by increasing the amount of CBM in preparation. CBM is definitely an internal application of power for rotation rather than an external one.

The Optimum Time to Lead Rotation!

Leading in Tango, or any partnered dance is extremely difficult. When leaders and followers learn that timing is much more than maintaining the general cadence of the music their dancing takes a great leap forward. As a beginner you will try to either lead or follow, keep the tempo, and progress all at the same time. Even if you were to do all of these three perfectly, doing them at the same time would produce a rough or harsh form of Tango. What the dancer discovers is the sequence of events that takes place in the designated period of time, or window of opportunity, that is known as, "timing." At the highest level of partner dancing, in which the dancer's technique is theoretically perfect, we judge his overall quality by the transitional moments from figure to figure. Any dance couple can learn complex dance figures or amalgamations early in their dance experience. It takes years to make sense out of transition; beginners please take note of this! Couple's egos often take over when enticed by "Fancy steps." Please be cautious when doing so. Only when both partners are comfortable in their transitions from movement to movement will your dancing be believable and visually agreeable. As a side note, you can actually spoil your basic beginning technique, by inadvertently developing bad habits in attempting to do something that is really too difficult for your stage of dancing. Muscle memory has no ability to assess whether or not you are doing something correctly. It just registers the feeling and can leave an indelible error in your technique! Now that I have your attention, I want to give you a key for transitional capability for rotation, "As the knees pass!!!"

"As the knees pass," is an expression that I use with great frequency. I often joke with my beginner students (of one to three years), in answering many of the questions I pose, to receive a grade of 90 percent simply answer, "As the knees pass." This information will serve you well in your dance experience. It is a key moment in the dancer's movement! At this moment the dancer's weight is about to change. It is the moment best suited for rotation in that their position has achieved the best vertical alignment and balance. Even a moment before this position has been achieved, to lead a partner into a rotation can be hazardous to her balance and the completion of the desired rotation. Work with your partner and discover exactly what the time of knee passage feels like. Then work your rotation. Rotation for the gentleman can be quite difficult for he must lead his partner to her rotation and then rotate himself. The real difficulty exists because he must finish his and set himself before his partner's rotation is completed. When the free knee (unsupported) passes toward and under the corresponding pelvis you have experienced knee passage. Each and every progressive dance movement experiences knee passage. Therefore, there is an appropriate time to lead and follow any rotation. You will find when

The Knees of the lady passing prior to the completion of a Back Ocho practicing this technique that you may have to slow down, or speed up, various aspects of your dance movements and configurations. This is vital to smooth transition and to greater clarity in the understanding of timing.

Foot Position in CBMP:

One of the important characteristics of quality dancing is controlling the movement of both feet at all times. I have mentioned previously that in the Argentine Tango you need to retain foot or toe pressure on an entry to the foot or exit from the foot when the body is engaged in progressive movement. In other words the feet do not leave the floor while moving from one spot on the dance floor to a position further along the dance floor. The Argentine style provides for a captivating momentary delay of foot speed while a progressive walk or stroll is in progress. This more than anything else gives this style of Tango its jungle cat or feline quality of movement.

In the American style of Tango, the feet are released from the dance floor on each progressive step. This technique clearly defines the major difference in the two styles of Tango! There is no delay in the feet once traveling has commenced in the American style.

Now that we have clarified the differences of foot movement and placement once again I want to discuss a usage of the foot and leg position that is common to both styles. We will call these positions, placing and or holding the foot in CBMP. CBMP are the initials for an important dance term. It is important to all forms of dancing. The phrase that describes CBMP is: Contra-body Movement Position of The Feet. This is not as complex as it sounds. When we move with CBMP the free or traveling foot crosses the plane or line of the dancer's body in the direction he is moving. For instance, the second step in PP (Promenade Position) will necessitate a movement of the foot with CBMP technique. In this case the free foot of the dancer will be released sufficiently from the dance floor to travel just slightly above and across the standing or supporting foot. Many new dancers do not know the desirability of releasing and stepping over the other foot as a technique in PP. The result of omitting this technique from a second step moving in promenade will be to force the couple further away from each other and possibly to create loss of balance and connection.

When placing the foot or holding the foot in CBMP it is desirable to make the first contact with the outside edge of the sole of your shoe. The outside edge being the portion of the foot that is farthest from your body's center. There should be a good amount of tone and pressure between the soul of the shoe and the dance floor. This pressure however, is not to be construed as a weight change or even the beginning of a weight change. It should be thought of as a

This is how the free foot travels in both styles of Tango

Lady's Forward Ocho while man holds his foot in CBMP

strong and beautiful leg line. Additionally, this tone between the foot and the dance floor will secure the partner who is leading a rotation such as a Fan or an Ocho. The lady who has completed a Fan or Ocho action will often finish her figure's movement in CBMP. This will then match the position of the gentleman's leg line.

The gentleman creates this leg line in CBMP when he rocks backward or replaces his weight backward during his lead for a Fan or an Ocho. He allows the former foot to stay in place at the point of the outside edge of his dance shoe. The leg will remain elongated and the outside edge of the foot will skim gently, to cross the directional plane of the dancer's body. Please see the photo as this position will be used with great frequency.

YOUR NOTES:

The Basic Dance Positions and Body Framing in The Tangos

To best understand the body and leg positions of both styles of Tango it is important to understand the general ballroom stance and body positions. I will describe the general ballroom stance and body positions numerically and then make comparisons using the description found at that number.

General Ballroom Frame Man's FRONT

The General Ballroom Stance and Body Position

are essentially parallel to the partner. Please note that in any of the following descriptions the dance couple must use the best approximation possible. Above all, comfort is essential in moving properly and maintaining balance for progressive and rotating movement. When there is a great height disparity between the couple the view of the shorter partner will definitely be obstructed.

1. Each of the partners will stand with his feet together. The feet of each will be facing each other's. The point that is formed by the toe of the **right** shoe will face the space between the partner's toes. The toes of the partner's feet will be no less than four inches and no more than six inches from your own. Please observe strong compression in the area of the abdominal wall. The contraction of the abdominal muscles will result in control of the upper body and lengthening of the spinal column. This abdominal contraction can be created by a strong exhale from the diaphragm. Breathing out or exhaling at rhythmic intervals will maintain this strong abdominal alignment while you are dancing. This abdominal control is essential to all forms of partner dancing including all styles of Tango. My discussion about CBM includes more about this topic.

2. The right foot of each partner is dead pointing at the line between his partner's feet.

3. The vertical center of the right thigh of each partner is directly opposite each other.

4. The right side of the gentleman's ribcage is opposite the sternum or vertical center of the woman's ribcage.

5. The right side of the woman's ribcage is approximately opposite the gentleman's sternum. Two partners would have to be exactly the same size for these reference points to be perfect, and that is unlikely.

General Ballroom Frame Man's BACK

33

6. The chin of the gentleman is in line with or pointing over the woman's right shoulder. This would be approximately between the edge of her deltoid and the center of her neck.

7. The chin of the woman is in line with or pointing towards the gentleman's right shoulder. This would be approximately between the edge of his deltoid and the center of his neck.

8. The elevation of the head must be maintained in any dance so that the centers of the ears are over the dancer's shoulders. The jawbone of the dancer's head should remain parallel to the dance floor and or the dancer's shoulders. The gentleman's jaw should be level (Parallel) with the dance floor with his gaze at his eye level. The woman's jaw be held at a comfortable level (According to her ability) above the parallel plane of the dance floor. Her gaze is above her eye level. If you were standing at one end of the room facing the other the level where the ceiling meets the wall would be a good benchmark.

The elevation of your head along with the gaze of your eyes are very important to your dancing, balance, and comparisons of one style of Tango to the other!!

**American Style
Dance Position**

The American Tango Stance and Body Position

Use the above general ballroom list by comparing one numeric description in that list of the general ballroom frame and body positions to the corresponding numeric description of Ballroom Tango frame and position. Begin by forming the general frame and physically make your comparisons for the Ballroom Tango frame.

1. The gentleman will stand with his feet approximately two inches apart. The ball of the right foot will be opposite the side of the arch of the left foot. The exact opposite will be true for the lady. These foot positions will accommodate forward and backward movements in CBM using CBMP. You will soon discover that the positions of the feet are natural to the Tango. They will inherently close to a position slightly in front of or slightly behind the other foot. Although the feet are very different from the ballroom foot positions, in the dancer's frame these positions accommodate easy use in Tango. Since the Tango frame is more compact than the ballroom frame it will not be unusual for the feet to be closer than the 4 inch proximity described in the ballroom frame. Additionally, the knees of the tango dancer are compressed inward toward each other. This also may be described by saying that the knees are closer together than the ankles. To practice this position a student may take a small throw pillow and hug it with the knees. While you are learning to dance the Tango, please maintain a feeling of flex in the hamstrings muscles while bracing the knees. Compression of the abdominal

wall in tango is a very important feature necessary to succeed at this dance. In addition to the contraction of the abdominal muscles as described in the general ballroom body positions, Tango requires an additional abdominal rotation. For the gentleman, his ribcage will be rotated slightly leftward from the center of his pelvis; and for the woman, the compression of the ribcage will be slightly rightward from the center of her pelvis.

These varying Tango body positions are used in creating the atmosphere and characteristics of this wonderful dance. These central body contractions and compressions will create the desired effect on your extremities. The feeling of center in the dance will give meaning to the usage of your legs, arms, and even your head. What may seem eccentric or extreme in the Tango at a glance, will turn out to be quite natural and the result of your good body positions.

**American Style
Couple in Promenade Position**

2. The comparative foot placements are as follows:
The right foot of the gentleman having been placed slightly apart and farther back than that of the left foot also is pointing slightly at the instep of the left foot. The lady will have placed her right foot slightly back from the plane of her left foot and like the gentleman will point the toes toward the direction of the left foot. You will feel and see, that the position of the feet and knees accommodate each other. The right foot of each partner is just slightly more to the left than the ballroom foot positions.

3. The comparative thigh placement puts the right side of each partner slightly more to the left than that of the ballroom frame. I would say in the approximate area of two inches. Additionally, the tango dancer should feel a slight rotation of both thigh muscles toward the dancer's center. The muscles found in the lower abdominal area create and hold the compression of the thighs and ribcage. This is done with a contraction or series of continuing contractions of these muscles. Again, using the theme of monitoring your own muscles, the dancer must continually correct and adjust muscles to maintain control for balance, speed, and rotation.

4. The line item numerical comparisons, found in numbers 4, 5, 6, and 7 are all more to the left for each partner. The degree of leftward position for the couple is contingent on the size difference between partners. The couple therefore will fall into natural positions somewhat more to the left than that of the ballroom positions.

5. The slight rotation described in number 1 produces a position that advances the right shoulder slightly ahead of the plane of the hips

for the gentleman. The lady will reciprocate by positioning her body with the left shoulder slightly back from the plane her hips produce. Once again the idea of torque or a twisting feeling should be felt in the abdominal area of both partners. In this text we have described the Tango walks and various movements. Some of these body alignments will become more important to become better at Tango. The elevation of the heads and the gaze will also be slightly more to the left than that of the General Ballroom positions. The difference owing to the comparative body positions will be somewhat more to the left.

The Argentine Tango Stance and Body Position

Argentine Dance Position

Use the former general ballroom list by comparing one numeric description in that of the general ballroom frame and body position to the corresponding numeric Argentine Tango's frame and position. Begin by forming the general frame and physically make your comparisons to the Argentine Tango's frame. The lady is generally rotated through her shoulders through to below her bust line much more rightwards than the general ballroom frame and she finds herself more right of the gentleman's center. Although the vertical position of her neck is secure, its elevation is slightly less owing to the declining and turned away characteristic of her head in Argentine Tango. This head position is well to the right in the basic in-line closed frame . Inclination of heads may actually move towards each other to the point of contact. This is contingent on the couple's skill more than their desire to be, "Close!" You will find that a larger space between you at first is a better idea until confidence is built between the couple. The poise of the couple is actually on the balls of the feet. The couple does not look at their own feet. Their gaze is projected towards the floor to watch and become motivated by another couple's feet approximately 8 feet away from them.

1. The gentleman and the lady will stand with their feet approximately two inches apart. The toes from one foot may point slightly towards the toes of the other with the weight on the balls of the feet. This will allow for strong and reliable compression through the upper legs. This greatly resembles the

body's carriage of the Latin Ballroom dances. Progressing in the Bolero or Mambo only occurs incrementally as is the case with the Argentine Tango. Since the Tango frame is more compact than the ballroom frame it will not be unusual for the feet to be closer than the 4 inch proximity described in the ballroom frame. Additionally, the knees of the tango dancer are slightly compressed inward toward each other. While you are learning to dance the Tango, please maintain a feeling of flex in the hamstring muscles while bracing the knees. Compression of the abdominal wall in tango is a very important feature necessary to succeed at this dance. Together, the flex in the knees and the compression of the abdominal wall will allow rotation to flourish by keeping the body active rather than passive while the feet are closed. In addition to the contraction of the abdominal muscles as described in the general ballroom body positions, Tango requires an additional abdominal rotation. The gentleman's his ribcage will be rotated slightly leftward from the center of his pelvis. The lady's ribcage rotates **leftward** from the center of her pelvis. This is all different than the Ballroom style of Tango.

Rear View of Couple's Argentine Style Frame

A note to the ladies: The opposition or contrasting positions of your shoulders verses your hips in this dance will definitely create some twist in your back. If you have any discomfort from attempting the normal position or from any of the figures, either consult your physician, moderate your position to a place of comfort, or do both!

These varying Argentine Tango body positions are used for creating the atmosphere and characteristics of this wonderful dance. These central body contractions and compressions will create the desired effect on your extremities. The feeling of center in the dance will give purpose/meaning to the usage of your legs, arms, and even your head. What may seem eccentric or extreme in the Tango at a glance will turn out to be quite natural and the result of your good body positions.

2. The comparative foot placements are as follows:

The right foot of the gentleman having been placed approximately two inches the left foot also is pointing ever so slightly at the toes of the left foot. The lady will do the same. You will feel and see, that the position of the feet and knees accommodate each other. The outside of the right foot of each partner will be exactly opposite each other. This is a placement much more to the right than the ballroom foot positions. A major difference in the Argentine style is that the weight of the body is poised over the balls of the feet while being compressed through the knees.

Couple positioned in Right Outside Partner Argentine Style

**Left Foot Stroll in
Left Outside Partner Position
Argentine Style**

3. The comparative thigh placement puts the right side of each partner slightly more to the left than that of the ballroom frame. I would say in the approximate area of two to three inches. Additionally, the tango dancer should feel a slight rotation of both thigh muscles toward the dancer's center. The muscles found in the lower abdominal area create and hold the compression of the thighs and ribcage. This is done with a contraction or series of continuing contractions of these muscles. Again, using the theme of monitoring your own muscles, the dancer must continually correct and adjust muscles to maintain control for balance, speed, and rotation.

4. The line item numerical comparisons, found in numbers 4, 5, 6, and 7 are all more to the left for each partner and closer at the upper elevations of the body and head. The chins of the couple will follow the gaze of their eyes. The degree of leftward position for the couple is contingent on the size differences from partner to partner. The couple therefore will fall into natural positions somewhat further to the left than that of the ballroom positions.

5. The slight rotation described in number 1 produces a position that advances the right shoulder slightly ahead of the plane of the hips for the gentleman. The lady will position her body with the left shoulder slightly forward from the plane her hips produce. Once again the idea of torque, or a twisting feeling, should be felt in the abdominal area of both partners. Some of these body alignments are very different from your normal day to day body alignments but will become more important as you become **better dancer** doing Tango.

Together with the framing positions of the arms and the body you should have a very good idea about the Tango dance position. These positions aid in giving this dance character. Although I have given great detail to both the arm and body positions, there has been one overriding theme to the Tango frame and that is the torque found in the abdominal wall. Given the compression of the pelvis upwards and the ribcage inward and down, the body positions in the Tango feel much longer as compared to the general ballroom dance positions. This is due to the compression of the lower abdomen and the knees.

A note to the dancer:

you will find throughout descriptions of dancing, viewing dancing, learning dancing, that there is the enormous potential for illusion. Our human eye will never see force or energy. The eye will only see the result of force or energy. Therefore we are prone in our evaluations to exaggerate and mimic the last thing we saw. The last item the eye saw was an extremity action some distance away from the center of the body. The extremity action viewed may be an arm, a shoulder, or a foot, etc. that has moved into a final position. However, our eyes did not register the cause of the positioning. The final position was simply the last thing we saw. As we become more experienced our mind's eye becomes trained to feel what we observe in dancing and movement. Without this evolving attribute it is difficult to perform new movements, patterns, etc. in dance. The human mind has great difficulty mimicking physical events and actions. The important point here is to begin your movements and energies at the center of your body. The frequency of abdominal contraction will ensure that you are beginning at your center. You will be amazed at how well the legs and arms move while at the same time the body remains quite still or controlled if you flex your abdominal muscles. Additionally the legs will swing with the characterization of the Tango again if you maintain the torque in your body.

This note to the dancer is important to both styles of Tango dealt with in this text as well as dancing in general!

The Arms and Hands:
Structure, Position, and Usage

The first item to remember is the **shoulders are always relaxed and positioned down towards the ribcage.** The muscles around the front and back of the ribcage will flex and provide a shelf for the arms rather than your trying to sustain the necessary lift in the upper arms with the shoulders.

The following technique is general and is useful for all forms of dance including both styles of Tango.

These two points are stressed because 999 out of 1,000 people when told to lift their arms into dance position will use the top of their shoulders as in shrug. This is wrong and can cause painful cramping if allowed to continue for any length of time. This incorrect use of the shoulders is the reason that new dancers often produce such a poor dance frame. The instinctive attempt to avoid pain in the shoulders results in the constant need to adjust the dropping arms and elbows. These constant adjustments must be made by the new dancer because he lacks the knowledge of the muscular creation of a good frame. A better idea is to learn how to position the arms and back into a solid position, like a shelf, that breathes or is still as necessary. I want to teach you the **correct** procedure to lift your arms and maintain a workable and comfortable dance position for Tango.

Stand with your arms freely relaxed and then pressed down from your shoulders. For an experienced dancer this often feels as if you are wedging your fingers into your underarm. With your good vertical poise and your arms loosely held from the shoulders your palms will hang in front of your upper legs facing the thighs. While flexing your abdominal wall as well as your pectoral muscles swing your upper arms from the shoulders until your elbows reach the elevation of your bust line or sternum. This should create a flexing of the muscle group known as the Latissimus dorsi commonly called the "Lats." Once lifted, rotate the area between elbow and shoulder (which includes the biceps and triceps) until they have created a 45 degree angle from their hanging position to the dance floor. Your elbows are then moved as far back as possible and yet remain slightly in front of your shoulders. This rotation will diminish the elevation of the Trapezius muscles also commonly called the "Traps," and will produce a long smooth shoulder line parallel to the dance floor.

Another important attribute that you will both feel and see the result of, is the opening or expanding of the underarm area. As the underarms expand you will feel an intensification of the upper back muscles. This procedure will complete the shelf for your upper body framing. One major result of this new framing technique is increased flexibility and rotation of the upper arms. It is very important to your dancing regardless of style or type that the feeling of openness in the underarm area is maintained. With the openness of the under arm area your arm speed and flexibility will be increased dramatically.

These are critical for when "breathing the arms," the dancer wants no inadvertent movement of the body. Inadvertent body movement that results from arm movements must always be avoided. "Breathing the arms," is a description that I use in my teaching to denote the condition of flexibility, connection, flexing, and response within the frame of the dance couple. "Breathing the arms" is done correctly when the transmission of lead and follows from within the couple is fluid. Fluidity will be felt within the joints and firmness within the muscles. In addition to lead and follow, "breathing the arms" will signify to each partner when their counterpart has completed a dance step. Practice will allow you to do this without the loss of balance, elevation of frame, or the need to look at the feet!

You will also notice that your neck looks longer and more elegant. This is very important to the appearance of a dancer. Longer appearance of the neck as it is held vertically will display your new confidence of body position as a dancer. You should find this new position to be relaxed through the shoulders and very firm through and across the upper back. Thus providing you with the ability to sustain your upper frame comfortably for several minutes at a time.

Check to see if you can swing your forearms from your elbows like a windshield wiper **without dropping the elbows** or the upper arms. The result of this arm positioning is the freedom to let the arms "breathe" or move when desired without creating inadvertent movement of the body. When the arms are positioned so as to be part of your standard Tango frame, they will be securely integrated into your back muscles and therefore your leading and following applications will transmit the correct messages.

Creating A Comfortable Hand Hold:

I want the lady to give the gentleman her right hand by placing the base of her palm (the area just above the wrist) into the center of his left palm. This way, as she closes her fingers gently, they will reach over to the back of his hand. The area of the gentleman's hand where the lady will fold her fingers is between his thumb and index finger. This handhold is comfortable and when he gets nervous or thinks intensely the woman's fingers cannot be squeezed to the point of turning purple. Please note that experienced dancers never clamp down tightly on their partner's fingers with the thumb or fingers. This clamping is more restrictive than useful. We need to

This concludes the general technique for the usage and positioning of the arms and hands. Now we will discuss the individual styles of arm framing in the Tango.

Argentine Tango's elevation and positioning of the hands

**Argentine Style
Position of Arms & Hands**

create an accessibility to all interior points of our partner's palm and fingers. The joining of our hands is always designed for both interlocking and quick release. Hand positions are never static, nor do they continue in the same position throughout a dance. Just as you can move around while talking on a telephone, so too must you be able to maintain this vital link in the physical communication of Tango. The leader will use both sides of his fingers in addition to his palm in a multitude of positions painting directional information on the canvas of his partner's interior hand and fingers. The trick in doing this is to always have the availability of the basic handhold at your disposal. As you practice, see to it that no matter what position you find your hands in (owing to the particular dance figure) you can instantly return to the basic closed position! In Tango the left (man) to right (lady) handhold finds the wrists of the couple a bit closer to the torsos of the couple than would be the case in the general ballroom frame. This allows for the natural generation of compression within the couple's frame. This will aid in the many promenade and circular movements you will soon discover.

Elevation of Hands in Both Styles:

The **Argentine style** has no specific elevation requirement for the couple's hand hold (his left to her right). The professional dancer concerns himself with the ability to maintain the elevation of this handhold, once the choice of elevation has been made. It is well known that in an earlier time of Tango's history the higher the handhold the greater the skill of the dancer and along with this the demonstration of his masculinity. For today's social Tango dancer I recommend the couple's handhold at the elevation of the mouth line of the gentleman. His left wrist is elevated slightly higher than the wrist of his partner allowing for the lady to project wrist pressure both vertically and horizontally.

Gentlemen, with the middle finger of your right hand, touch the woman's back at a point on or below the elevation of her shoulder blade and to the left of her spinal column (from his perspective). The placement point of the middle finger of the gentleman will differ from couple to couple. The region of the lady's back where this placement will occur is between her waist and the elevation of her shoulder blades. The disparity exists because of size differences in couples and how closely they choose to dance. The wrist of the gentleman will be slightly below the elevation of his elbow. Do this without compromising your upper arm position. With respect to Ochos where the leader must assist his partner through rotation, he will find the need to use either the base of his palm or even his wrist (contingent on his skill level and the figure type) in contact with the lower portions of his partner's ribcage.

The **Argentine** style will find the woman's left hand generally coming to rest on his right shoulder or just below the gentleman's shoulder cap (between the biceps and the deltoid). In this style of Tango the arms of the woman will move around this general area. Remember there must be freedom to create the desired position and communication. This then becomes a general guide because there are no static positions in Argentine Tango.

The **American** Tango is specific in its elevation of the joined handhold of the couple. This handhold levels itself at the eye line of the lady. At this elevation the index finger of the man is parallel to the dance floor. The lady will join her right hand to his left as described earlier in the general technique. Gentlemen, with the middle finger of your right hand, touch the woman's back at a point below the elevation of her shoulder blade and just to the left of her spinal column (from his perspective). The placement point of the middle finger of the gentleman will differ from couple to couple. The disparity exists because of size differences in couples. This position is slightly advanced rightwards from the general ballroom position as described in Quickstart To Social Dancing. The wrist of the gentleman will be slightly below the elevation of his elbow. Do this without compromising your upper arm position. The triangle formed between the neck and each shoulder, and from elbow to elbow, should resemble a coat hanger. With respect to Fan type action where the leader must assist his partner through rotation, he will find the need to use either the base of his palm or even his wrist (contingent on his skill level and the figure type) in contact with his partner's left rear corner of the ribcage.

The woman has some choices in the Tango regarding the placement of her left hand to conclude the couple's frame. The **American** style of Tango allows for three popular arm and hand positions. After having placed her elbow in contact with his upper arm 1) she may place her left hand on the gentleman's back just under his right underarm, 2) just below his right shoulder, 3) or inline with the tricept muscle. Comfort and size relationship to her partner will dictate which of the three she uses. It may be wise to change this position from partner to partner rather than remaining uncomfortable while dancing. All positions breath better for the American Tango when the palm of her left hand to faces the dance floor.

American Tango's elevation and positioning of the hands

American Style Position of Arms & Hands

Compression within The Frame:

The last important point I want to discuss is the feeling of compression within the dance couple's frame. This compression is felt neither as pushing nor pulling on the partner. A better interpretation is to feel the compression of an accordion. One might also compare the feeling of the frame to that which might occur if you were to hold the trunk of a big tree or the carton from a new refrigerator. I like to compare the couples frame to the creation of a large rib. The ribs, as you know, proceed from the spinal column away from the dancer's center thus creating width. The ribcage creates the depth of the body. It extends toward the front center of the body. In like kind we want to feel separation and width from our spine with our upper arms. I like to feel stretch of the Latissimus dorsi to and through the elbows thus creating as wide a wing span has possible. Energy from my back then is transmitted through to the elbow and then the wrist, culminating at the center interior palms of the dancers' hands. When both partners do this a circle of continuing energy is created that completes a powerful connection with their partner. Any rotation felt through the body is transmitted with reciprocity to the partner. As a matter of finesse the couple strives to diminish the intensity of pressure while learning to increase the capacity of connection. "Less is more."

There are so many circular movements and rotations particularly in Argentine Tango these arms must breathe properly and quickly without loss of connection. Breathing arms, a term that I have used several times, deals with the flexibility and speed of the contractions or expansions of major joints. These joints from the shoulders to the hands must operate on demand without impedance of any kind. One important note requires reiteration, the dancer should rotate the ribcage whenever possible rather than allowing the elbows to proceed behind the shoulders from the perspective of the body's plane. The erroneous relaxation of shoulders to the point where the elbows go behind the body's plane will be eliminated as your dancing improves. The new feeling will include the use of torque by your body created from positions of CBM and rotation of the rib cage.

Important note: Through the Quickstart exercises you will learn that the arms will have to move in conjunction with each other. This will insure that rotation led through the gentleman's body, will be felt through the lady's body. Any rotation continues through her body to her standing foot. This is very important to the construction of the couple's connection in both forms of Tango. Gentlemen mere twisting at the waist or moving one arm at a time to lead your partner will not produce the desired effect in your Tango. Connection must be retained at all times!

Congratulations, you have now become the single entity known as a dance couple!

44

Attitudes and Priorities: Mental and Physical

With Yourself:

Now that you have decided to learn to dance do not make comparisons to your present station in life, economic success, educational experiences and related degrees. These must not be used to challenge your own ego. One might say, "I have been successful in all else; this to will be easy. " But by doing this, you are setting yourself up for a big fall! Equate learning to partner dance to learning a basic physical skill with another person who does not speak your language. Since you cannot verbalize with each other, you must discover other means to transmit information. There is nothing "Heady" about this communication. It is quite elementary in nature and strictly physical. Therefore your mindset must return to the days of your youth. Those days of learning to ride a bicycle or learning to swim will best suit your attitude in learning to dance with a partner. The difference is then your partner was a bicycle or the water. Now your partner is another human being. It was exciting to see that new bike or swimming pool. Although they were inanimate objects, they were to become your new friends. You planned to spend countless hours of fun with them. You dreamed and planned for this. Then came the reality check. You had to learn to partner them to fulfill your expectations. For a while your new friends seemed to be your new enemies. A while passed and you learned to appreciate the quality and inherent capabilities of your new partner. You learned, and the fun began! Although you loved your new bike or swimming pool, your love for these inanimate objects was only shared by one, you. Your dance partner can reciprocate that love and every other feeling that you feel as you learn to dance. Unlike the perfection of the water or the engineering of the bicycle your partner is very human, like you, and imperfect. They, like you, must be tooled into a dancer. The dance couple is something you both will work to create. It is a new entity and does not as yet exist. Intellectually, emotionally, and physically you are going to learn a new language, and your muscles are going to teach your brain a new skill. **That skill is partnering.**

It is easy to underestimate the difficulty of partner dancing. We can watch two people just like us execute a dance, and two others really execute or destroy a dance. As an individual or solo, our mindset and all we relate to are singular. We watch a dance couple make many maneuvers on the dance floor that by and large resemble little more than walking forward or backward. We say to ourselves, "Look how easy that is! I can do that." Yet, when we walk no one is attached to us. Our movements are free and easy with absolutely no encumbrances. We have no thought about our posture, length of stride, or speed of movement. All we have to do is get to the destination and we have been a successful traveler. Many people have danced what we call freestyle or solo dancing. We enjoy this footloose and fancy free form of dancing in front of a partner. Moving to music is great fun. It is emotionally charged, particularly when dancing to our favorite song with our favorite partner. As a solo dancer, you are dividing the difficulty by at least three, as compared to the difficulty of a dance couple. The good news is you will be able to multiply your solo pleasure by much more than three.

With Your Partner:

Previously, we spoke of treating yourself kindly. Now let us address the issue of our attitude toward our PARTNER. To negotiate properly we need two partners; first, either someone to lead you or someone to follow, and secondly the music that becomes a partner to both of you. Without the music and its sensuous interpretation you and your partner cannot dance.

I find the dominant personality of the couple tries to control the other partner. Frequently this ends the dance or partnering relationship. Remember a couple in partner dancing is really a singular animate object. The attitude and personality of each of the members make up a component of the dance couple but should not dominate it. If your arms dominate your legs, you cannot walk. They must exist harmoniously. Whether you dance for the pursuit of excellence or just for sheer enjoyment, dancing will bring you to one threshold experience after another. The point being, to achieve even a moderate level of success in any form of partner dancing both partners will have to face the same trials and tribulations. At the top of the mountain both of you will experience the same joys of achievement and pleasure. Each member of the dance couple must really do some soul searching to understand this and then allow for each other's frustration, errors, growth, and adaptation to partnering and partner dancing. Neither member could possibly know it all (nobody does). You could not possibly know how you feel to another person. How could you? A clone of yourself would have to exist with a complete and a continuous transmittable sense of feeling. You are trying to become a perfect building block or that certain piece of a puzzle that fits just right.

Be very kind to your partner and remember you are learning too. Consider this when you attempt to teach them or "just show them what to do." You are taking responsibility for knowing what you are showing them, "cold," or as an expert. Now what your partner executes in their dancing is your doing. More often than not, this can become your undoing. Because you are not an expert you can only correct your partner with a negative. An example of this would be, do not do this or do not do that. Maybe you let your parents get away with negative criticisms, but your partner is not your mother or father. Parenting your partner without authority will generally produce a negative. An experienced dance instructor knows how to issue a positive command that has the effect of eliminating the error. This takes many years of good dance experience and then training as a teacher or educator of dance. Sometimes the definition of an expert is as follows: In mathematics "X" is an unknown and at our sink's faucet, a spurt is a drip of water. Do not become an unknown drip of water when working together with your partner! Consider the amount of time you have spent learning to dance. Relate this training to an hour by hour experience to see if you are an "expert" or the unknown drip of water known as an "X- Spurt."

There is no question that you will learn at different rates of speed; nobody is the same, and you are learning different things. Be prepared to learn to walk all over again. I would estimate three to four times more qualitatively than your present gate. You must not let this bother you. In order to dance, this metamorphosis must occur.

You will, and I mean -- will, hit road blocks. You will also achieve many rewarding threshold experiences that will more than offset your struggles and failures. Be very prepared for this and treat yourself kindly. Make no assumptions about how easy or difficult partner dancing may be. You have had no experience with formal training at this form of dancing. As you embark on this adventure called partner dancing, please enjoy all of your growth. Many others with fewer skills and tools have tried and learned to dance successfully. I promise you will too!!

With Your Muscles:

While you are dancing your feeling throughout the muscles of your body will become a monitoring device. Without the ability to see what you look like on the dance floor this inherent monitoring of muscle position and contraction will be your new set of eyes. Work with a mirror on these positions to familiarize yourself with what they look like and of course the way they feel. In this way no one will have to tell you how you look while you are dancing, performing, or competing. Some of you may not like the use of the mirror initially, but make friends with your appearance. I always tell my students that if they do not like the way they look through the course of their dancing, it is likely that others will not like how they appear either. The reason for this is that we convey attitude, feeling, confidence, as a window of self expression and emotional feeling. When you become familiar with these various feelings, the usage and control of your muscles will cause your confidence level on the dance floor to soar! These familiar feelings will be like an old friend that you have not seen for a while. That old friend always gave you a good feeling after your encounter with them. There is a positive net result in using muscle memory to control your dance positions. You will exhibit greater control with respect to your torso, legs, and arms. Your concentration will be focused toward where you are going on the dance floor along with your partnering skills and transitional capabilities. Dancing is the personification of music. Concentration on your musicality and movement across the dance floor is essential to express the art of partner dancing.

Relax! It Is Good Food for The Muscles:

As long as you keep that great attitude you will be feeding all the muscles in your body very positive information. All muscle usage begins with electrical impulses deep in the brain's central nervous system. A chemical known as ATP (Adenosine Triphosphate) is released to the muscles. It acts like a food or vitamin. When you get tense it burns the food. Burnt food is too crisp, hard, and overdone. The ATP is supercharged with heat and will cause the joints operated by certain muscle groups to stiffen and react differently than you planned.

Your muscles will not perform anywhere near their capability. In other physical activities and sports, athletes refer to this as "CHOKING." Once stress or anger has invaded your practice time, stop! The stress will cause your efforts to be totally counterproductive.

New Choreography

Here is an a mental and physical approach to learning new choreography. Foot pressure is generated only when your body is vertically aligned in a position over your foot. This is a dance step! Some poor folks believe that the simple act of putting your foot somewhere per directional instructions will do the trick. That type of foot action is merely a tap or touch, not a dance step. These sometimes argumentative folks are never going to learn quickly enough to put them at ease. For one moment please visualize the beach or a swimming pool. What do you do when testing the water temperature? Why of course, you dip or tap your foot into the water and at that moment have no inclination to move forward into the water. The act of **tapping your foot** out to the water **produces** a stiffening or **holding** action in your body **preventing movement**.

Similar placement of your foot will never produce movement on the dance floor. That pathetic student who tapping his foot without committing his weight is still arguing with the Laws of Physics. He will become very frustrated with his negative learning curve. They may try one or two more lessons and then quit. He will tell others he just cannot seem to get it or that he did not like the class or the teacher.

Simply stated, this student used the wrong body tools as an approach to learning dancing. Please, please, please do not join him in his obstinacy and failure.

To learn new choreography commit your entire body to the step as an approach to learning. Do this with a positive mental attitude as if you had been doing the new step, figure, or position for years! Never be afraid to make errors when you are learning something new; it's how we train our muscles. Errors will only remain errors in your dancing if you persist in repeating them. Once you have discovered the use of proper techniques from your practice or exercise patterns, make sure you apply them to any new dance figure or choreography.

Your Practice:

It is important during the course of your practice to set realistic goals for that particular practice session. In that way you will become success oriented in achieving your designated goal. If you are able to surpass your goal, your practice time will also have become motivational. You will look forward to your next practice with great affirmation. Part of goal setting should include bringing your dance figures, patterns, routines, etc., to the speed of the music. If you only attempt to perfect your dancing at a very slow methodical pace, when you introduce music to the formula it will be very, very discouraging. A better idea is to add the music soon into your practice. The lack of physical perfection in your new dance amalgamation should not deter you from adding music. These two major entities, the physical and the musical will merge quickly. You will find that there is a great disparity in performance with and without music. This is very normal!

To deal with the music in your practice session I feel the following sequence will be helpful. Give attention to each physical movement and transitional skill, along with the leads and follows. Do this for a single figure or a short sequence of figures. Add the music once this practice has been accomplished. Then connect your new choreography to a basic pattern or a preceding pattern and continue to practice them in succession. The development of a routine will include the use of the 'adding-on idea.' Keep the new figure at the end and start your material from the beginning. Dance your existing material to the point of failure or weaknesses. Rework the weaker material and start from the beginning of the routine. You will be surprised at how many, 'mountain top,' experiences you will have. The older material will be executed with great confidence and familiarity. Therefore your attention and concentration will be focused on the new material and you will get through it sooner.

Achieving A Higher Level:

In your goal setting there is a reality of which you must be aware. You will never dance better than the level of your best practice session! Never deceive yourself into believing that you will dance better when the pressure is apparent. The truth is your public performances, at whatever level, will include any and every mistake, weakness, or insecurity, that exists in your practice sessions. Most highly skilled professionals are elated when their performances or competitive dancing achieves a level of 85 percent of their best practice. Your practice session must include achieving the 100 percent level of your physical capability as frequently as possible. It is this 100 percent level that you are trying to improve upon. To achieve a higher level of dance in a public venue, competition, showcase, or performance, you will have to practice an increase of your capacities. This must be done at the 100 percent level! Practice sessions held in a public venue such as a nightclub or social dance floor will not produce the desired results and may become discouraging. There are too many negative variables to contend with to use this public practice as your only form of practice. Do your homework at your own pace and in privacy. Remember, this privacy will always produce your best practice. If you do not have space at your residence for private practice, it is a good investment of time and money to rent space somewhere for an hour or two. Think about it and you will find some accessible public hall.

The following is a check-off list for your use in concluding our discussion about attitudes:

- You must treat yourself and your partner kindly and patiently.

- Please be cooperative and encouraging. Strive to maintain equality.

- Eliminate all negative emotion from your learning and practice time.

- Do not practice when you are exhausted or have just eaten. This will be counter productive.

- Once you have planned what you are going to practice endeavor to practice at the one hundred percent or, 'full tilt,' level.

- Get your dancing up to the speed of the music as soon as possible.

- Set realistic goals for each practice session.

- Above all, have fun when you are learning to dance. Remember, this is not brain surgery or life threatening!

Tango's Social Development:

A Collaboration by Jeff Allen
and Daniel Trenner, founder of The Bridge To The Tango

Around 1875 Argentina experienced an unprecedented population explosion. An immigration began that lasted through 1920 resulting in an exponential net of ten times its original base population. The immigrants came from every country in Europe. Argentina's original cultural community prior to 1875 was virtually obliterated and certainly fully absorbed within the span of 45 years. Ninety percent of these new settlers were male. At the turn of the century in Argentine gatherings it was not unusual to have one hundred men to one woman.

Resultantly, a women's role in this society was highly defined. The first role generalization would be one of cultural taste and always in the presence of a chaperone. These women were never found in the company of male strangers and remained insulated from all but a close family circle throughout their lives. The alternative for the remaining women was within the subculture of prostitution and crime. The proportions of the populace made it all but impossible for a woman to find a different path during that period. The competition among men was based on their ability to earn money and attract women.

One of the few places that a proper girl could be courted was at a social dance. The traditional social dance was a folk dance made up of traditional European Waltzes and Polkas. The men who attended any of these social dances had no chance to learn at them. A girl would only consent to dance with the most experienced of the gentlemen who were present. This presented a paradox for the males of this period.

For men the center of social life in this period was the male rooming house. It was called the Conventillo and was built around a courtyard. Here the male social life would take place after work. A fair comparison to a barroom or nightclub could be made. The men would drink, play music, and dance with each other. They would practice Waltzes and Polkas for the purposes of respectable courting.

Musicians were experimenting with a new folk music and the male dancers were developing a parallel counterpart. This dance was called the Tango and was classified as lascivious because the bodies of the dancers were pressed together while the legs of both the male and female were thrust at each other. Occurring at a time when even exposing the lady's ankle from beneath her petticoats was considered too risqué for a refined woman, this dance sent shockwaves through respectable society This simple walking closely with a partner and nothing more, was the scandal of the new dance.

The disproportion of men versus women made the brothel a very popular place. Occasionally, these same musicians were hired to perform at the brothels. The men from the Conventillo with some money to spend would join in this new form of music and dance while waiting for service. The pastime at the brothel was typical of a house of prostitution and not of a dance studio. This setting was a stage for fantasy and storytelling which would of course include this new folk dance. The romanticism of this history becomes myth when it is thought that the Tango was the lure to the brothel.

A parallel development of the Tango was occurring among the Oligarchy (upper class) of Argentina. Rich young males clandestinely appeared amid the lower classes at the Conventillos and at what we would call the "Red Light Districts" of the city to "Sow their wild oats." They were exposed to the Tango at the brothels and the Conventillos. The custom of the time was to send the rich Argentinean male to the cosmopolitan city of Paris, France to gain continental refinement, exposure, and education. This was like a rite of passage and the young man would stay there for as long as three years. The Tango went with him.

Around 1910 the Bourgeois (middle class) in Paris were very liberal and there was an intense cabaret scene Amongst the cabaret productions was what we would call "Black Theater," and its portrayal of a thug or gangster of Paris. They called this production and its protagonist an, "Apache." This term was first used in 1902 by Victor Moris a French journalist who wrote about the Parisian thieves. The portrayal of an apache included handling his woman in a brutal and masterful way. This becomes important to us because these young men from Argentina befriended the cabaret performers and began to develop what became a dance known as the Tango Apache, with a similar brutal male dominant theme. This Tango Apache became the source for the Tango craze in Europe and North America between 1910 and 1920. Additionally, the men returning to Argentina brought with them this form of the Parisian influenced Tango, and it became the choice of the aristocracy. Once home, these young men had no further access to the French cabaret performers, they called upon their local musicians and dancers of the Argentine Folk Tango to instruct and entertain them in the ways of this new dance. From this integration of styles, Folk and Apache, began the development of the social form of what is now Argentine Tango. The fiscal collapse of Argentina during the depression created an economic and cultural separation from Europe and therefore the dance began to evolve dramatic differences from the European and American Tango.

The similar rooting of the tango ended in the 1920's between the North Americans, Europeans, and Argentineans. By 1930 and through the Golden Age of the Tango in the 1940's most Argentineans has accepted their unique form of tango and, in relative isolation from the rest of the world, it continued to develop its characteristic idiosyncrasies. From the 1930's onward the same footwork between partners occurred known as, "Crossed Feet." This technique is used with such frequency that it is characteristic of the Argentine style while it is only hinted at in the very advanced levels of American Tango.

The Golden Age of Tango was the period during World War II when Argentina's declared neutrality allowed her to sell beef to the rest of the world. Thus their economy prospered. Once the war ended the Perón government was overthrown. Under a horrible dictatorship the country returned to a depressed economy and a repressed society. The Tango and its artists either went underground or left the country. Democracy returned in 1982 and the Tango found its way back to the clubs via the senior citizens who had danced during the Golden Age. A phenomena occurred; some youngsters left the disco scene and fell in love with the Tango of the 1940's for it had not changed. Their study, work, and perseverance of the original forms of Argentine Tango resulted in the Broadway production of *Tango Argentino* and the current Broadway show *Forever Tango*.

This history must step back for a moment to Tango's development in America. Dance professionals, most notably Vernon and Irene Castle (A stage name they used based on their, Castle Walk) were intrigued by the Apache Tango and soon developed a form of Tango that combined the caricatures of this Apache dance together with the progressive movement of American dances like the Boston, The Turkey Trot and Mr. Harry Fox's new Foxtrot developed for the Ziegfeld Follies in 1913. The dance was banned in Boston but caught on like wild fire in the greater New York City area. On the first day of 1914 The New York Times reported , "ALL NEW YORK NOW MADLY WHIRLING IN THE TANGO". And, if you were to visit my home state of Rhode Island at that time, the mansions of Newport would have provided the venue for America's new Tango. The Castles taught the new American Tango to the very wealthy at fees of up to $100.00 per hour and obviously at much less to those who were interested more in the dance and not just in the art of name dropping. The Tango quickly spread throughout New York's dance studios.

Broad based national acceptance of the Tango came when Rudolph Valentino danced with Beatrice Dominguez in the 1921 film, The Four Horseman of the Apocalypse. Valentino had been a cabaret dancer and interpreted the Tango, as the others had, from the Parisian Apache Tango. Although the Tango purists may not have welcomed Valentino's caricature of the dance, none can deny the influence that one scene had. Studios throughout America were teaching the Tango to thousands of dancers and curiosity seekers. Hollywood has never been the same since.

Tango's Theatrical Development:

The History and Lore of The Tango

THE TANGO: A DANCE, A CULTURE, A WAY OF LIFE

Although it has come to epitomize the glamour and elegance of high society, with women in sleek glittering evening gowns and men in tux and tails, the tango originated in society's underbelly--the brothels of turn-of-the-century Argentina. As immigrants from Europe, Africa, and ports unknown streamed into the outskirts of Buenos Aires during the 1880's, many gravitated toward the port city's houses of ill repute. In these establishments the portenos, as they were called, could drown their troubles in a few drinks and find some companionship. They looked desperately for a distraction to ease their sense of rootlessness and disenfranchisement as "strangers in a strange land."

From this heady, intermingled cultural brew emerged a new music which became the tango. Though musical historians argue as to its exact origins, it is generally accepted that the tango borrowed from many nations—the relentless rhythms that the African slaves--the candombe--beat on their drums (known as tan-go); the popular music of the pampas (flatlands) known as the milonga, which combined Indian rhythms with the music of early Spanish colonists; and other influences, including Latin. Some say the word "tango" comes from the Latin word tangere (to touch.) Ironically, as these lonely immigrants and societal outcasts sought to escape from their feelings, they instead developed a music and dance that epitomized them. The wail of the tango, it is said, speaks of more than frustrated love. It speaks of fatality, of destinies engulfed in pain. It is the dance of sorrow.

Originally, the tango dance developed as an "acting out" of the relationship between the prostitute and her pimp. In fact, the titles of the first tangos referred to characters in the world of prostitution. These tango songs and dances had no lyrics, were often highly improvised, and were generally regarded as obscene.

THE TANGO: A DANCE, A CULTURE, A WAY OF LIFE

has been reprinted with permission from the Website

(http://www.forevertango.com/index.html)

of

Luis Bravo's Forever Tango appearing on Broadway at the Walter Kerr Theatre,

218 West 48th Street, New York

Further, the early tangos not only represented a kind of sexual choreography, but often a duel, a man-to-man combat between challengers for the favors of a woman, that usually ended in the symbolic death of an opponent. Sexual and evil forces were equally celebrated in this ritual. During this time, the wailing melancholy of the bandoneon (an accordion-like instrument imported to Argentina from Germany in 1886) became a mainstay of tango music.

With the advent of the universal suffrage law--passed in Argentina in 1912--the lower classes were allowed to vote. This served to legitimize many of its cultural mainstays, including the tango. As it became absorbed into the larger society, the tango lost some of its abrasiveness.

The structure of the dance, however, remained intact, and soon the tango developed into a worldwide phenomenon. Even the Americans were doing it, although some ladies were given to wearing "bumpers" to protect themselves from rubbing a bit too closely against their male partners.

During the first two decades of the new century, the tango took Paris by storm. The blessings of the Parisians, in turn, made it a staple of Argentinean high society. Tango was reigning supreme in the cabarets and theaters frequented by the rich. Out of this culture, the tango musician became elevated to professional composer status.

A pioneer in this genre, Roberto Firpo, created the typical tango orchestra—rhythm played on piano and double bass; melodies played on the bandoneon and the violin, with strong counter melodies and variations. The stars of this era were Osvaldo Fresedo and Julio de Caro.

In 1918, lyric writing for the tango become the latest trend, bringing forth the birth of a star who is still celebrated five decades after his death—singer Carlos Gardel. The memory of this handsome, charismatic performer has reached hero worship status in Argentina, not unlike what Elvis Presley inspires in the USA.

In 1930, a sudden military coup in Argentina ended the citizens' right to vote, and thus largely silenced the voice of the people, the tango. During this time, a very pessimistic philosopher/singer of the tango emerged, Enrique Santos Discepolo. He is famous for the line, "The 20th Century is a trash heap. No one can deny it."

Tango revived in the late 1930's when the Argentinean masses regained a good measure of their political freedom. They celebrated their social rise with the tango, which became a symbol of their physical solidarity and part of their daily life. Again, tango musicians emerged who took the form in new directions including Fresedo, de Caro, Pugliese, and Anibal Troilo.

56

Soon, wealthy intellectuals, far removed from the working class, "orilla," began writing new lyrics for the tango. Because of their influence, tango took on a more romantic, nostalgic, and less threatening air, a sweet remembrance of youth in an idyllic society that never existed.

When Juan Peron rose to power in 1946 the tango reached the pinnacle of popularity in Argentina, as both he and his wife Evita embraced it wholeheartedly. Yet, with Evita's death in 1952, the tango again fell from the mainstream spotlight. American rock-and-roll invaded the popular scene, and the tango again seemed out of step with its times. Today the tango is enjoying a renaissance of popularity, keeping the fire of this daring art form burning brightly.

This internationally acclaimed dance spectacle arrived at Broadway's Walter Kerr Theatre (218 West 48th Street) on June 16, 1997 and due to its box-office success has been extended indefinitely as an open-ended run.

Tango Impressions:

The following vignettes are here to stimulate your beginning and continuing study of Tango. They will mean more and more to you as you grow in knowledge and ability. Please return and read them often particularly when a spark is needed for inspiration, motivation, or enlightenment. Enjoy!!

TANGO: WITH FEELING:

It took many years and just the right partner to achieve what I believe to be the perfect tango attitude. We were always on the same wave-length and heard the music in the same way. He was a very powerful, experienced dancer that I always knew I could rely to "be there" for me in a tight situation.

Because of this non-verbal communication we could be playful with each other and the dance. We believed that the tango is the quintessential conversation between the Gentleman and his Lady partner. It is his attempt at subtle masculine control over her, all the while the Lady is "allowing" him this illusion. While utilizing her feminine wiles to the maximum, she will always make up her own mind, all the while having him believing it was all his idea in the first place. The conversation goes something like this.... Gentleman, "Yes, she will!" Lady, "No, I won't! ... Well, maybe..."

SANDRA LEE WOLLIN - EMERSON, NEW JERSEY
Professional Ballroom & Latin American Instructor, Author

TWO PRACTICE SESSIONS:

"1989, Buenos Aires - Practice at Canning; It is after the practice but before the dance. My partner and I have the place to ourselves and we are dancing with enthusiasm.

An older fellow is at the bar, quite drunk, and he comes over and tears me away from my partner saying 'Daniel! No es asi!' ('Not like that!') He leads me around as the woman for two dances, lights go off in my brain. They have talked a lot about how men used to learn with other men, but in the coed world of modern Argentina it never happens.

So I hire the guy to teach me some privates. We lead and follow each other. I've learned from a brute how to lead like a brute and, though I've made a big leap in understanding, my partners are not pleased.

1990, Buenos Aires- Practice at Joachim V. Gonzalez: I meet Juan Bruno, 70, 'the kid from Ciudadela', who sees me dance and says that what I don't understand is how lead and follow works.

He proceeds to lead me around the floor softly, sweetly, looks up at me, winks. This time I've found a gentleman, my partners approved of the results, and I've never looked back. To lead like a gentleman follow one."

DANIEL TRENNER - YARMOUTH, MAINE
creator of Bridge to the Tango (Catalog, Events, Instruction, and Tours)

A Conversation:
between Carlos Gavito and Jeff Allen

Jeff: Carlos, dancers are athletes. Why Tango and not football *(soccer)*?

Carlos: That is a good question. I never mix sport with dancing. Sport is an enjoyment, a physical enjoyment. Dance, is a spiritual enjoyment.

Jeff: Very good, a lot of people would have answered, When I play football I'm out there with the boys when I'm dancing I'm with a woman!

Carlos: I don't think that they are related. Totally unrelated. It's the same as being a ship's captain or a plane's captain. It is a trip that they both travel. It doesn't mean that they are the same thing, the same feeling, the same experiences. They are altogether different, not the same. In football there is the speed and strength and the purpose is just to hit the ball and try to make the goal. In tango the longer it takes the more I enjoy it. So really, in fact, I don't want ever to finish! It's not related one thing to the other.

Jeff: So there is no perfection in tango. It's always evolving?

Carlos: Perfection, yes. There is a lot of perfection in tango. Perfection in tango is when you make known your work to really work the right way always. But you first work many days, day by day to make it better so it is a perfection you reach, or try to reach, day by day and you're never right. With great perfection, yes. Yes we try to get perfect but never quite get there.

Jeff: I know the feeling! Every student of dance has a mentor or a role model. What is the one piece of information that you continue to pass forward from your mentor to your students of Tango?

Carlos: I always say we should learn, and I think I learn from the people who teach me. So there is a space of generations and learning from experience. And always I say, in my country, and I was a boy when I heard these words, "You dance Tango on the beat of the heart," Holding his chest affectionately in the area of the heart, Carlos repeats, "Tick tock, tick tock, tick tock and that is the heart beat."

Jeff: Do you remember who told you that?

Carlos: No, those were words from anybody in those days. Especially in those days of the 1940's, let's say, which was the "Golden Era of the Tango," in my country. All the most experienced dancers, orchestras, and singers of Tango, let's say they were in the age of their success in those days in my country. Tango was a success in my country in the 40's to 1955, so I knew a lot of people who could be my grandparents' age. They gave us, not only me but people like me, the experience, the knowledge, the understanding of Tango. As I say, generation to generation. In those days we do not have television. We have football during the day and Tango during the night! *(We both laugh strongly and Jeff says "That's why I asked you about football!" Stronger laughter by both!)* Yes, very much our fashion and our wisdom to love - with the football and the boys in the day, yes, and with the girls in our arms in the night!

Jeff: There we go. That's what I was talking about! *(much more laughter)*

Carlos: So now the answer comes in a different question. The answer might be the same, but the question was different.

Jeff: So you were Dancing Tango when Eva Perón was in power?

Carlos: Oh yes, I was just starting to learn. Here is a funny story of when I was starting to learn. But I always tell it because it is true; that's why I can remember it. When I was a kid, just a kid seven years old, the backyard of my home linked with the center, what we call the "Apple of The Block," It was the center near an empty space and that empty space linked to the two clubs in my town. One was on that street and the other around the corner. There were two walls that were linked to the "Apple," and I had to jump one wall and then the other wall. And I was in either one of the two clubs, when my mother thought I was sleeping. So really, I jumped the wall when I was 7 years old to learn the Tango.
In those days that was pretty funny because the way we learned Tango was a game. Yes, sort of passing through the ball. We got the football and the oldest passed the ball to us. In a way like saying, "Hey kid come here. Stand here. Let me see how I can do that step." And they

put us in the position of the girl, and they played. And they do steps and fancy things and we were sort of the pigeons, the experiment. That lasted to the moment I reached my fourteenth birthday.

In those days 14 was when you received the long trousers, when you could start to dance as a man, not before that. So then I started to do the same until I was 19 years old. I would call, "Hey boy, come here. Stand here. Put the feet here. Let me see how I can do that."

So, that's the way we learned Tango. You must understand in those days it was hard times. If you were wealthy there was only one well known school of Tango, Gayita (sp), but only one. The rest could not learn Tango through a school, or go to a dancing school. We learned Tango just in the clubs. You know, in the streets between friends. Never were there girls. We learned the hard way. We learned as a girl and then as a man to lead. That's why I say always, "I lead but I follow." So I lead a way, but I follow her, so I never have toes on her.

Jeff: Many times I teach my students the same way. I make the man learn to feel what the lady has to feel so he can transmit the same feeling.

Carlos: Of course. He has to feel the same understanding and the same security to make her understand what he really wants. I say always, "They don't have the crystal ball. So somehow you must make them understand what you want to do." *(Jeff: Another language!)* Tango is another language, a body language. I would say an intentional body language. Sometimes it is intentional. Some times just a gesture and a look to the side make your move to her. Then you really stand up, and then you show her more. I try that in my classes, and we have a good fun always; because if she knows I'm just going to do just that , she is going to move the foot to the side. You must try that, and you will see. *(Although seated, Carlos was making simple gestures with the tips of his fingers while looking away from the corner of his eyes and making a very slight body inclination)* So that has the meaning, to me, swing foot and how you move you the body intentionally. The body should lead a person even without moving yourself.

Jeff: When I was teaching Whitney, *(Whitney Brown, my life and soul mate, was present throughout this wonderful conversation)* Tango she used to laugh. She would never believe that it would come out of her. *(Carlos is chuckling while glancing at Whitney)* She always thought people were making it up.

Carlos: No, no, no, no, no, no, (he says softly and rapidly with a smile at Whitney) Have to come out a lot from her. A lot it has to come out from yourself. And again, if I lead and I follow you, it means I allowed you to do whatever you want. And I follow you so I will never be on your toes. I will wait for you to move first. So that's why sometimes I might move just intentional my chest going forward without moving my foot. That will allow her to move the foot first, and I follow.

Jeff: I tell my students a story. I say it's like life. You can show a lady where to go and you can suggest a place But then, you must follow her there.

Carlos: Definitely. Absolutely, absolutely true. Absolutely true, absolutely, 100 percent. If you are teaching her, and without pushing, we embrace!

Jeff: All right we are having too much fun. What was your most important Tango professionally, other than the Broadway experience? What was a turning point in your career?

Carlos: Ohhh, hmmm, I got so many. First one occurred in 1967 when I started to dance in an orchestra in Argentina. Very well known and to me my glory! *(Jeff: what was the name of it?)* Miguel Caló, a singer which I most admired myself, my hero. And that guy make me form a duo because he knew me from the dance. He said to me "You should prepare a duo, and I will present you." That's what I did, and he kept his promise. He took me to "Patio Tango," on Corrientes Street which was the "Tango Avenue" where it all happened in Tango. Like Broadway in the show business. Corrientes in Buenos Aires is a jewel in a way specific to Tango. And I went there shaking like a leaf. I was really shaking. I was 22, 23 years old, and they say to me, "OK you prefer dancing on the stage or we'll make a space on the tables and you'll dance on the floor?" Because the stage was a high stage, I say I prefer to dance on the ground, in the basement, *(we all laughed loudly)* because I was so scared.   So he tried to humor me. He decided to treat me another way, "No, no. Come. Don't worry. If you dance on the stage, I'll be right beside you." I was with that orchestra for 6 months.

Now the second occasion, ah is so hard to say. I have hundreds of occasions. Second occasion, I went to Columbia first time. To the Festival of Tango in 1968. With another orchestra very well known, Aníbal Troilo. This was also a tremendous emotion. (Note from author: the list could have been endless. Carlos seemed not to want more importance placed on one than the other. They were all great strides forward for him! His statement at the end of this who's who in Tango says it all: "My goodness, my dreams!")

Jeff: So, if I ask you, what was the most emotionally and meaningful Tango that you've ever done?

Carlos: It's everyday! Everyday!

Jeff: Everyday?

Carlos: And I never know when is the best. No I'm lying to you. No, to me dance every night is a different experience, is a different feeling, a different emotion, a different reason. It's a different way to listen to the music. I hear sometimes a little thing which I never heard before. I say, "How come it was there?" And then I move my finger, a finger, a finger! I say, "I never do that before!" No, no, to me it's everyday a start. And as I say before, and it's not a joke, I want always to keep in my mind dancing. The word Tango never ending. If it is today, or for years, I would be…. well maybe it is a little fantasy, but it's like you don't want it to end. Ending is a sadness, I don't want that. I want to enjoy! Did I answer that?

Jeff: Absolutely, absolutely, I fully expected that answer.

Carlos: That is a bridge from my heart, I don't mind if you write that I don't care. I'm telling you that is something that comes from inside!

Jeff: OK, my last prepared question *(all laugh):* The pinnacle for every performer is to perform on Broadway! How does it feel? And how has it influenced your art?

Carlos: Yes, it's a funny thing. Yes, it's been perhaps, I don't know, many years, wondering when I will be on Broadway sometime. "Oh my goodness, if I could get to Broadway." And when you get to Broadway, then you say "What else is there?" There's nothing else. It means Broadway ,for us artists or dancers, it is just one more step in our life; but the life doesn't end there, and we pretend much more than that. So, I'm very happy. Listen, if you think about it, I've arrived. Broadway when I am 55 ,and some arrive when they are 23. So, I don't think it is a question, to arrive. It's a question of how do you arrive? With what knowledge and what experience in life? And how do you enjoy to arrive to Broadway? I think I am very satisfied. Feel beautiful. I feel great. I feel, eh, I think, I'm in my peak of my life. It's the peak! I think perhaps I start to go down now, I don't know. But now I know, I'm in the peak of my life! I hope no. I hope I get somewhere else to work, maybe Hollywood!? *(All laugh)*

Jeff: And its influence on your art?

Carlos: Rehearsing, performing, which is like I say I didn't land here and that's it. No, I want more, so I don't want it to end. I want to keep going. I don't want that to end.

Jeff: Has it changed your dancing or teaching at all?

Carlos: No, No, No, No, No, I go on the stage the way, the same way, I dance. Dance for demonstration, and I teach that. I'm very strict about that!! I'm very perseverant. I'm obsessed, and my pupils they know that.

Jeff: Are you a tough teacher?

Carlos: Yes!

Jeff: I'm a tough teacher!

Carlos: And a very good one! *(Carlos laughs, Jeff laughs)*

Jeff: Try to make the pupils respect the art!

Carlos: Yes, yes, yes. Listen, that is very, very important. Listen to me. A student would say " We are not dancers" Listen lady, from the moment you step a foot, you are a dancer. That's a dance floor. If you don't feel like that, then get the hell out of here! Because if you want to put your foot there , you are insulting me, if you say your problems. Because that's a dance floor. That is not a shop, a market, a café, a restaurant. That's a dance floor. So from the moment you decide to put on a pair of shoes and come and put a foot there YOU ARE A DANCER. I'M GOIING TO TREAT YOU LIKE A DANCER!!! And I want the same response. I want you to be a dancer!!

Jeff: I feel better now!

Carlos: You must, you must, you must have that mentality. I hear many times comments about things and it's funny. I think as dancers we are a very strange kind. In fact, I believe we are as a dancer a little masochistic. We take a dance class and if we go out without feeling a pain in the muscles, I don't come anymore. I didn't work my body. But if you work me oooh, ahh, *(Carlos mimics being in pain),* I say son-of-a-gun. I come next week and I kill you!! You see, we want to feel if we are working, that our bodies are working which is really doing what we have to do.

Jeff: Harvey Edwards is a world famous photographer. Predominantly of the Ballet. He had a beautiful poster image that I used to have in my first studio. The studio burned down *(Carlos: Oh God)* the poster burnt up. "If it looks good it hurts!!"

Carlos: No question. Definitely. It's that little more which you don't do because you are lazy that is very important to show in dancing. Some people say, OK I know how to stretch a leg so I will stretch it easy. No. When you take a class you stretch the full leg. No half way through. You go for the maximum. So when you dance *(perform)* you do half, maybe. If you do three pirouettes on the studio, you do one on the stage. It's not the other way around. There are people who think if you can do three in the studio, you can do six on the stage. Oh, no way, no way. If you do three in the studio, you do one on the stage; and you will do perfect. And if you do two maybe. If you do three, you're gone. Because you do easy at the studio.

Jeff: We never achieve our best practice!

Carlos: Never!

Jeff: Never

Carlos: Never, but how many times did you rehearse and you did a full routine complete, without mistakes?

Jeff: It's not possible!

Carlos: I never did in my life!!

Jeff: It's not possible!

Carlos: And if I ever do something good in rehearsal, surely when I start again something is wrong. Something is wrong. I don't know why, but it is the mind, the body, which doesn't work the same time. Rehearse. That's why you rehearse. To make the mistakes and then to secure *(correct)* the mistakes; that's rehearsal.

Jeff: Every mistake that exists in your rehearsal will show right up!

Carlos: Absolutely, absolutely! *(Whitney turned to both of us, "I don't want to take the class if you two teach together!" We all laughed and embraced!)*

We concluded our conversation with a deep sense of warmth, and new found friendship. I know I learned much from this Tango virtuoso, Carlos Gavito. I hope my readers find this conversation an inspiration to your Tango! As a side note, Carlos seemed to be looking out for me that night, in the audience, and saying: Did I perform as I represented myself? My answer, Yes, Carlos, you did!

**CARLOS GAVITO -
PERTH, SCOTLAND & NEW YORK CITY
The senior member of the
Broadway cast of Forever Tango
and also teaches Tango in New York
and around the world.
Carlos is pictured with Marcela
Duran**

Argentine Tango

Figures in Argentine Tango are done socially are like a conversation, one never knows in advance the exact content of the conversation, just the topic, you and your partner. Each conversation has an opening and an ending with a little or a lot of dialogue, contingent on the intensity of the topic. Another contributing factor is the interest of the conversationalist regarding the topic. In dancing the Argentine Tango passion is expressed as partners make their intentions and desires known to each other by a series of responses and even challenges. It is even possible for other couples to influence a conversation. One couple as an onlooker may "ease drop" on another couple's conversation and become inspired or even "turned on!" They are choreographically inspired and react by changing the course of their conversation with additional foot patterns. This is how they learn!

In addition to progressive movements there are also responses created by using dance figures and leg gestures know as, "Adornments." No other dance in a basic form rivals Argentine Tango in creating a language of desire through the use of limbs as a means of expressing this language. The figures have come symbolize of the many moods of love and the way lovers travel this path with each other. It has become clear to me that this style of Tango is much more than a dance. It speaks of a present and past history of love and events.

The dancer takes the knowledge of what has gone on before him and adds his experience to create a Tango. We improve the physical and spiritual levels of our love making with time and experience, so does our Tango. I feel Tango music is generally masculine and would interpret the music danced to the American style as being quite aggressive and macho throughout, while the Argentine style music is smoother and very romantic. This style like the dance takes much more time to tell a story. We would call the Argentine style music more leggiero (which is smoother, lighter, nimbler and much more connected. I have mentioned earlier, the American Tango music is very staccato (shortened at the early moment of the musical beat).

We have discussed the essential walking movements in Argentine Tango, previously in our text. You will find much information with respect to control of the body head and legs in The Movement and Control Exercises for Tango. Rotation and torque are exceedingly important in the successful leading and following of the Argentine Tango. Once you have grasped the image of a figure type below, return to the exercises and techniques to work your way through the patterns. I have presented figures that I feel will entice you to fall in love with this dance. They are not difficult, for difficulty would frustrate you. They are rather a Quickstart To Tango, that you may continue to be educated in this dance by a competent instructor in your area.

A Physical Philosophy and Logic for Argentine Tango:

I want to introduce you to a physical philosophy that will serve you as a template for Tango. It will become the basis for the logical continuity of your Tango dance. Once the dance couple is in frame the leader must depend that **our partner will travel backwards** using a slow rhythm as a standard. The leader has the responsibility of changing the course of direction and use of figures (we call this floorcraft) of both his partner and the couple. As the follower walks backwards there is an invitation created. This invitation says pass into my space, visit me here, speak to me! The follower says, "If you stop, I'll turn around to revisit you." The action of stopping and facing your partner while she continues to travel will become an Ocho. The result of his stopping while she is turning places the leader at the center of a circle. If the leader chooses to move forward or backward, she will logically resolve her rotation and begin to move with him. Her continued commitment to walking backward then becomes the progressive movement of a back walk.

The leader may take another course of action. He may incrementally move sideways as his partner resolves her rotation. The result of this sidestep will become a turn know as a Giro. The leader rotates to accommodate the continued and committed progressive movement of his partner while she begins to circle him in a grapevine. The grapevine action around the leader at the center or hub of a circle, is a logical outgrowth of his incremental but non-progressive rotation. The circular grapevine is an integral figure to the Argentine Tango. Here we see that an Ocho becomes a Giro when sidesteps are taken.

At any time the leader may reverse his direction allowing for the logical conclusion of his partner's weight change. This will be resolved with a rotation based on **her philosophy** of a committed **back walk**. Once again this rotation will become an Ocho. His continued rotation at the center at the hub will produce a grapevine figure. This process continues at the whim of the leader.

The leader's intermittent and rhythmical changes of direction may give the follower or himself the opportunity to pause and use Adornments to accentuate this physical philosophy. The level and type of Adornment will measure the growth and expertise of the dancers. In this text we will mention some Adornments but be more concerned with the fundamental construction of the Tango.

The leader may begin to step out of this center at a time of his choosing, while allowing his partner to resolve her rotation. She is committed to movement backward and begins to travel. The space created by the follower's invitation allows for the leader's movement inline or to the left or right of his partner. The leader will frequently, with experience, change from parallel feet to crossed feet. Crossed feet will engage the partner with a variety of opportunities to Adorn that would have otherwise not existed. If the leader is progressing and moves to the right outside partner position (his right leg between his body and hers) with CBM in place, the follower will feel the beginnings of rotation. As a result of this right outside partner progression with CBM, a crossing of the feet will occur rather than an Ocho.

Line of Dance (LOD) for Argentine Tango

We must observe line of dance (LOD) when dancing in public! LOD is the counter-clockwise traveling direction a couple uses around the dance floor. The Argentine Tango will accommodate any of the dance floor conditions that exist during your Tango. Your dance progression needs to reflect the population of dancers on the floor and the space available. Tango patterns such as the Stroll will move you to available space. Dancers who find themselves in the midst of many other Tango dancers or in small surroundings must restrict their movement. The use of rotating figures such as the Ocho or Giro will accommodate these conditions.

My recommendation to couples who are just beginning to Tango is to stay toward the extreme edges of the dance floor. Those that want to demonstrate more flash and rotation please move to the very center of the floor. This will allow those who travel moderately to have an assessable inside track for some progression and some rotation.

Always remember you should never dance a figure for the figure's sake if it will impede or bump another dance couple! The leader looks where he is going while paying attention to his partner. I always tell my students jokingly I will split the difference with them, the left eye for LOD and the right eye for their partner. Remember if you really wanted to dance into the floor then look at it, otherwise look where you are going, it is a marvelous concept!

Please return and reread this physical philosophy often for it is the basis of the Argentine Style Tango as presented in this text.

The Choreography of Argentine Tango:

Left Foot Stroll In Line with partner—Ball of foot contact

Your Vocabulary for The Dance

The Stroll (el Paseo) was detailed in your Quickstart moving exercises. It is the most versatile traveling figure in Argentine Tango. The stroll will progresses in several ways with your partner. The dancers are moving **In line** when traveling in their normal dance frame. We will also Stroll in what is known as outside partner to Ballroom dancers or Out on the Right Stroll in Argentine style. Traveling, Out on the Right Stroll, occurs when the gentleman moves in CBMP with the lady to his right (his right leg between him and his partner). Another transition occurs when traveling with partner to the left of the leader (his left leg between him and his partner). This is know as outside on the Left Stroll (the gentleman moves in CBMP with the lady to his left). As mentioned previously in my physical philosophy, your skill and versatility with respect to moving begins with the follower's commitment to a backward Stroll.

The execution of the Stroll was the major basis for developing the stalking walk exercise. It may be wise to review Movement and Control for Tango before going on! Think of the various forms of the Stroll as a life skill rather than what appears to be a very simple dance step. Strolling with a partner in your arms is not simple. You must endeavor to improve your basic walking skill every day you dance! It is the barometer for the solidarity of your frame, center, and base. Endeavor to use your foot as long as possible before exiting. This will enhance the directional clarity of the dancer's movement. This additional time spent on your foot will produce the best musicality, balance, and control, in your movement!

Accuracy in the directional movement of your body is the key to good partnering skills. Just one moment prior to moving the bodies backward, lightly and swiftly swing your thigh backward so that the big toe of your foot touches the floor behind you.
Please remember that to begin any movement the knees must flex slightly. This will make sure your entire body begins to move as you commence to dance. The lady is also alerted by this flexing action as to when the gentleman is about to begin. Make no mistake about it this movement together with the controlled cadence of the music IS dancing. Please count aloud while practicing to insure you are moving harmoniously and in a synchronized fashion with your partner. An example of this would be: 5, 6, ready (7), and

Right Foot Stroll Right Outside Partner Position

69

**Right Crossed Foot Stroll
Left Outside Partner**

**It takes three
strolling steps to
move from Inside to
Outside on the
Stroll.**

(8).   The key to a good beginning is to bring the body into action quickly with a very strong dance frame. You must make sure the Atlas & Axis (the joint) at the top of the spinal column moves at exactly the same speed as the Coccyx bone at the base of the spine. You must be able to maintain control of the entire spinal column in a position that is perpendicular to the dance floor. Never bend or lean sideways at the waist to start to Tango. **The body will not travel well in any linear direction if there is body rock or sway between the waist and the shoulders.**

Timing: Any Strolling step may be counted as either a Slow or Quick. It may be wise to work on perfecting the Slow rhythm first.

In & Out on a stroll:

When the couple is dancing Out on a Right stroll the leader will find his right leg between him and his partner's. The couple's bodies move in the streamline fashion known as CBMP.

The dancers are In on a stroll occurs when he returns the couple to their normal In-line closed position. These are to be thought of as transitional walks linking one figure type to another. The technique I use for moving in and out on a stroll highlights an increase of leg speed while reducing the pressure in my frame. This allows my elbows to breath within the constancy of a normal frame. I must also employ CBM owing to the fact that there is a slight rotation that occurs with the body. The leader's elbows are breathing when the follower's feel a widening of my frame not only in my arms but across my upper back. I am signaling to my body and my partner's that a form of rotation is coming. This greater width through my body can be compared to an expensive sports car, in that, the greater the wheel base as compared to the length of the vehicle the greater handling and response. In doing so I get a faster and even response from my partner while actually doing much less than those who are sloppy with their frame. Using this technique, I can graduate from any former position to in or out on the stroll.

As the name, Stroll, suggests there are no abrupt movements from positions in line to either in or out of the stroll. If I want to move in CBMP to either outside position I diminish the space between my forearms and biceps. This is done by increasing my leg speed and moving in CBMP. The leader proceeds with either the right side of my body for In on a Stroll or the left side of my body for Out on a stroll. Remember when leading in tango use the shoulder, upper arm, ribcage, and hip in conjunction with each other. Moving from In-line to outside a partner is an attempt to diminish the overall width of the couple's basic frame and not the individuals. The net effect in these positions will be in ease of traveling to and during rotating figures. They inherently give the couple more freedom to use, and increase the utilizable and workable length of their arms. A visualization of Out on a Stroll: In a normal frame a couple would not be able to move through a narrow door frame as he walks forward and she backwards. Once they have achieved the Outside position they can pass through the same narrow frame. The elbows and shoulders will pass through the opening before the necks and heads of the couple.

Crossed Feet in Argentine Tango:

There are essentially six positions that create opportunity for figure type, variation as well as improvisation. To retain the authenticity and characterization of Argentine Tango there are three positions in frame with your partner that we need to discuss. The first three of these six positions have already been dealt with.

They are in line with our partner, right outside partner, and left outside partner. These first three positions are done with natural opposite foot work. That is to say the leader's left moves with the follower's right. This is the natural or logical way that two people must use to move with and in front of each other. In ballroom dancing this is known as, **"Natural opposite,"** foot work. In the Argentine Tango this is known as, **"Parallel,"** foot work.

Crossed Feet Right Outside Partner

If we stop with **Parallel** foot work, we have limited ourselves to less than half of the opportunities that this wonderfully improvisational social dance affords us. A good friend Daniel Trenner, who conducts tours regularly to Buenos Aires. Mr. Trenner who is an excellent instructor in the Argentine Tango has conveys the importance of teaching **Crossed Feet** (both partner's changing weight to the same foot in harmony) at this early stage of development. **Crossed Feet** is actually more essential to the authentic social style of Tango than just the use of parallel feet. Daniel relays with a smile in his voice, that those who dance with just parallel feet are often the subject of ridicule by the more experienced dancers.

Crossed Feet increase the variety of entrance and exit opportunities to virtually all Tango figures. Crossed feet are synonymous with the usage of **"Same Foot"** terminology in ballroom dancing. The use of crossed feet, although more difficult at first, will ultimately provide greater enjoyment and conversation with one's partner during the dance. Crossed foot adds the remaining three positions for the dance couple. These three positions are **crossed feet in line**, **crossed feet right outside partner**, and **crossed feet left outside partner**. At the beginning stages of your Argentine Tango experience it will typically take three weight changes to move

71

from outside partner to in line with partner and then outside partner to the opposite side. This will help your dancing to remain smooth and non-rushed.

Now that we have dealt with what crossed feet are, I must help you to learn how to create the opportunity for the same foot application, while the dance is in progress. It is quite easy to start a dance with crossed feet. The leader only has to insure that the follower and he are standing on the same foot. This of course will be accomplished when the frame is in place for the couple and then through a breathing of the leader's frame. This response should be identifiable from the partner, by creating compression on the desired foot. The leader must reciprocate by placing themselves on that particular foot. An example would be the supporting foot of both partners would be the left, leaving the right foot free for movement. The beginner couple should commence their Tango with Crossed Feet. Dance to music in the Crossed Foot position and make friends with Crossed Feet.

The worked at hand is the ability to move to crossed feet and then return to parallel feet while in motion. I will convey what I do in these situations to help you practice and become competent and adapt to the same foot application. I will deal with two primary methods of creating crossed feet.

1. **Delayed leg speed**: this simply means that while my partner proceeds to change weight from one step to the next I delay the speed of my foot placement. What this does is create the crossed feet. It is hard to say that this takes exactly twice the duration of time but you may use that as a bench mark. The leader would have had to close the space between himself and his partner to allow for a breathing of the frame to a normal position. This allows for his partner's body flight while he delays his leg speed and ultimate foot placement. Practice, practice, practice is required to accomplish this with security and regularity.

2. **Holding the position of the foot**: The leader will learn through experience the opportunities to stay on their present foot while allowing their partner to change weight to their next foot. This opportunity generally exists when a figure pattern has brought the dance couple to a standstill with respect to bodyflight. Many of these foot changes occur when the figures incorporate rotation. Ochos and ochos done during the Giro are examples of this opportunity. Once again practice, practice, practice, without loss of patience or without frustration. Frustration only leads to tension physically as well as mentally and tightening of the joints and muscles result.

Sensitivity is required in the accomplishment of foot changes to crossed feet. The leader must develop the sensitivity and skill to feel the partner's weight change as transmitted through the couple's frame. Looking at a foot change is not learning or feeling the foot change to crossed feet. The elements of compression and sensitivity are required with great regularity in all of your dancing in addition to this application. The partner must be secure in their leg with compression after the impact (see: dynamic duo). This allows the leader to be secure in the physical knowledge (not visual) of the foot that holds the partner's weight.

Sensitivity: With a breathing frame the leader will also allow for this type of physical communication. The leader should never stiffen joints of the extremities. This subsequently holds the energy in these extremities the lines of communication are cut off. This is similar to a garden hose with a kink in it no fluid can pass through the hose.

I stress the geometric accuracy in your linear directions. The free leg must pass under the corresponding pelvis. When the action of knee and ankle compression occurs the knee must always move toward and then over the corresponding big toe. The follower must maintain the attitude of the natural movement and placement or continuance of their natural movement and placement of feet.

Now you have the full 6 positions relative to your partner to practice with great regularity. It is my feeling that this crossed foot action like its counterpart the parallel foot action becomes a "Life skill for Argentine Tango."

You must continue to achieve and grow in the Tango. It is the act of getting close to perfection that is important. This will require much practice but will unlock many doors of pleasure in Argentine Tango. Practice the three weight change scenarios from outside, to in line, to outside partner with both parallel and crossed feet. The timing varieties with crossed feet are similar to those with parallel feet. Good luck!

**Man closing on
Balls of both feet**

The Chassé
this figure is a one step pattern either forward, backward, or sideways followed by closing the feet to a side by side position. It is also a linking and leading figure. It is particularly useful when leading a partner to a figure type that is different from the leader's participation.

The follower may be rotating while the leader is localized to a stationary position. A single ocho or a closing action while creating a crossing action in your partner is examples of this. You will also use this side-together or together-together pattern for changing directions of the ochos when the leader is the hub. The together-together pattern is a marking time technique that is used in another very popular Spanish dance known as the Paso Doble. In both dances we use this step to mark time and fill or complete phrases of music. This type of step in Tango is known as la Cadencia, The Rhythmic Step.

Timing: Like the steps of the Stroll above the timing can either be Quick or Slow. I would however suggest that you do two of them at the same tempo for the time being.

When taking a side step followed by a closing action you will find it desirable to enter the foot at the inside edge. To exit the foot, you will use the inside edge. The inside edge is the side of the foot closest to the body's center. This use of the **inside edge of the foot** helps to create a smooth soft action that can not be attained if the whole sole of the foot is placed down at once.

Closing the feet in social dancing and forgetting to change your body weight to the closing foot is **definitely the most common error** in any type of social partner dancing. You begin to exhibit the instincts of a dancer when this error no longer exists, how ever it takes mental and physical concentration to overcome this. We always change weight automatically when the body travels from one location to another. Our brain instinctively senses the need to move the body to the next foot when the body starts to travel. This is part of the software that we were programmed with at birth. All you have to do is watch a baby learning to walk to realize this is true. When the baby's parents call the baby, the child attempts to move from one foot to the next. No one can possibly teach the baby to do that! The brain however, senses no need at all to change weight to a foot that is swinging to an ending position under our body but is not causing any bodyflight or movement. **Therefore there is no instinctive need to put the body weight on the closing foot.** The following technique will give you some helpful insight into the process required to make closing the feet where a weight change is required an instinct natural to your dancing.

74

Technique for Closing and Crossing The Feet:

Three things must happen in sequence when you close or cross the feet. All three happen on typically one beat of music.

a) The swing or placement next to, crossing behind (knee cap touching back of knee), or crossing in-front (back of knee touching knee cap) of the supporting foot,

b) The transfer of weight to the moving foot after the swing and placement of the closing or crossing foot, and

c) The release of the former supporting from the floor.

As a result, my recommendation is: Whenever closing the feet do so without the least bit of hesitation. Simply said, "As quickly as possible." This technique requires much practice.

In Argentine style, **while crossing**, the knees will be braced to a fully extended position or mildly relaxed from this position contingent upon the speed and quality of the dancer. It is very important to convey complete support to your torso while crossing. Simply stated, if you do not support yourself your partner will have the unpleasant task of doing so! This is a quick way to lose a dance partner or make a potential partner uninterested.

The Rock Step or Cradle (la Cunita):

This figure is nothing more than a change of direction without changing the facing position of the couple. If the leader is facing LOD prior to the Rock, he will remain so at its conclusion. The Rock step is used for easy transition, hesitation, or for good floorcraft La Cunita may be done Outside Partner in CBMP or In-Line in the basic frame. La Cunita may also be done in tandem with another rock as follows: Forward to a forward rock, back to a back rock, back to a forward rock or forward to a back rock.

To retain the characteristic of the Tango walk allow the knees to collect under the corresponding pelvis. To create a very attractive leg and foot line you may hold your foot in CBMP from the former position (See: Rotation In Tango). Take a walk forward and collect; then take a walk backward and collect. A note to the leader, you must maintain a constant speed throughout your spinal column and frame to lead any rock or replacement figure. La Cunita may be repeated forward or backward and may be initiated from either foot.

Timing: La Cunita is best done if both steps are the same rhythm. Therefore use either Slow, Slow or Quick, Quick.

Lady Crossing Her Feet

Man rocks back to his right foot

75

My personal experience and growth with the Salida as a sidestep!

The Beginning Pattern:

Until now, we have dealt primarily with steps that comprise the basic movements of the social dance known as the Argentine Tango. In keeping with the physical philosophy I have presented earlier in this section I want to continue with the figure that Argentine social dancers use to begin their dance. This figure is known as "The Walk to The Cross." This particular combination of four dance steps begins with a SIDESTEP.

I want to combine some of my own history (It is the one I know best) with the evolution of a more practical way of dancing. In mid-1985 the highly successful Broadway Show *Tango Argentino* came to New York City. By the end of 1986 learning to dance Argentine Tango was the rage of not only New York City but professional dancers and teachers, like myself, from all over the Northeast, US. In February 1987, Montreal, Canada I was competing in a major professional dance competition. I competed in the Open International Latin Division along with professionals from all over the world. One of the professional divisions was know as Exhibition Dancing. The couple from New York that won that year did a theatrical Argentine Tango. I decided I wanted to add elements of the Argentine style to my Professional Open American Tango. Cast members from the show *Tango Argentino* had already visited Montreal and had trained some of the teachers there its style. Since, there was nowhere to use this dance socially, we as performers and competitors were only interested in the "Theatrical Version" of this dance. Its social application in the U.S. seemed of little value. Frankly, until approximately two to three years ago, I held this feeling.

Since I was in Montreal for my usual dance training I decided there and then that I would learn Argentine Tango. We started with a few basic steps before getting into the "flashy stuff." I distinctly remember saying, "Oh no, not another dance that begins with the (man's) right foot, its a good thing we won't have to teach this to students!" The International Style of Paso Doble starts with the gentleman's right foot.

The instructor had shown me a basic pattern consisting of 8 steps he called the Common Basic. The first three steps took the form of the letter "U." The steps were; back on the man's right, side to his left, and forward right outside partner. It was perfect for the place in my American Tango we wanted to insert the Argentine material. I learned much later that these three steps of the Common Basic had a name, Salida (This is the entrance to the dance, although it literally means, exit or outlet). We started with the Salida and went on to some very advanced choreography from there.

My competitive Tango routine also doubled as performance piece that was warmly received, particularly the Argentine portion! As time passed, I taught the Argentine Tango upon request in private instruction. There were ice dancers as well as competitive ballroom dancers who availed themselves of my coaching in the Argentine style. I never taught this form of Tango as a social dance! I had always felt it was too obscure and would not be well received here in the US largely because of the right foot start of the gentleman!

For over five years I have been researching and writing my books about various aspects of social dancing including the American and Argentine Tango. As part of my research, I have been teaching classes in Tango and evaluating the learning curve of my students. I have always told them they were part of a research project and their reactions to teaching style and material was teaching me. Two years ago I began sense a growing tide in this country of social dancers doing the Argentine style. I attributed most of this to the new Broadway Show, *Forever Tango*. This is partly true but moreover, a new wave of dancer's from Argentina and American dancers who visited there where teaching Americans a truly social form of the dance. This included a **Salida** that began with the Gentleman's LEFT FOOT rather than the more theatrical styling that evolved from the first wave of show dancers from Argentina.

Now I was teaching two forms of a Salida. Without exception, those pupils who when exposed to the left foot start to the side, learned faster and had less confusion with orientation and acclimation. Students who were formerly exposed to the right foot back Salida and then the left foot start to the side, adjusted quickly and seemed relieved.

The relief seemed to be focused in two areas. The first was Americans are used to starting their social dancing with the gentleman's left foot and as a result the normal resistance to change. The second and more convincing argument for change are leaders do not have eyes in the back of their heads. No one can really be comfortable with a backward start. A consensus opinion from students and other professionals is to go with what works. I heartily recommend to other teachers and students who have, like myself, been exposed to the "U" shaped Salida (with the right foot start) to experiment with the socially palatable left foot to the side. This then becomes the first step of the pattern known as The **walk to the cross**.

**Walk To The Cross
Step #1
Left foot to the side**

77

The Walk to The Cross (La Cruzada):

This is generally a four step pattern that if taken as your first step in the dance includes what is known as the Salida (This is the entrance to the dance, although it literally means, exit or outlet).

The first step is taken with the leader's left foot. He must prepare himself to step outside partner (previously described in the Stroll). As a beginner you may wish to think of this as a side step slightly forward in a diagonal direction. When the first step of The Walk to The Cross is concluded the leader should have developed CBM in his body to prepare for Right Outside Partner Position on the next step.

The second step of The Walk to The Cross will be taken with the leader's right foot in CBMP which becomes the Right Outside Partner Position. His partner will walk back on her left foot. As previously described in your Tango exercises the product of CBM and CBMP is to produce some torque or twist in the ribcage.

While Right Outside Partner Position is maintained at the entry to the third step that would be the left foot forward for the leader the crossing action for his partner should be eminent. Therefore the continuation of Outside Partner plus the CBM alerts the follower both, mentally and physically for the crossing action.

The final two steps to complete The Walk to the Cross, making a total of four steps are the forward step Outside Partner with the leader's left and a close with his right foot. The follower does in coincidence the natural opposite foot in the following fashion. She moves back with her right and crosses her left in front of the right as described in the former crossing technique. The follower then releases her right foot just a moment after she has achieved her fullest moment of rise. Her crossing action may be a firm or soft crossing action owing to the speed at which it is being danced. The follower has now experienced rise in her Tango. Many of the movements in the Argentine style have incorporated into them rise and fall. By contrast to the American style of Tango that has no rise or fall. In many instances the action of the gentleman creates the rise for his lady.

We will observe that the lady brings the back of the knee of the free leg, to the kneecap of the standing leg, while she stands on the balls of both feet. This is what we would call a locking action and is one of the examples where there is rise in the Argentine Tango followed by the lowering action commonly referred to as fall. From an

Walk to the Cross Step #2
Right Outside Partner
with Right Foot Forward

Walk to the Cross Step #3
Left foot forward in
Right Outside Partner

intellectual standpoint I dislike the word FALL its connotation seems to indicate loss of control.   Dancers know that we must control our balance at all times! I will succumb to the common usage of the word FALL in dance nomenclature but please always remember that we are using a **controlled lowering action.**

Where there is a locking action needed through the lady's knees the leader must observe the technique of CBM and CBMP. He may increase the locking action's tension, or diminish it, by speed changes in his CBM and its amount of rotation. I remind you that you are not twisting your partner, the rotation begins within the leader's center and is resolved in the follower's center.

Solid legs evolve with rise to the crossing action and flex to the lowering action. When She lowers from any crossing action the body must definitely remain supported by the standing or supporting leg. She must take the compression into the thigh muscles so the lowering and progression to the next foot is controlled. She must contact the dance floor with her toe with a good deal of tone before she takes her body weight into the traveling foot while skimming slightly on the floor. This then completes the four steps of The Walk to The Cross.

Timing: The Walk to The Cross may use various rhythms It is hard to say what is the most popular. My favorite rhythm is Slow, Slow, Quick, Quick & The step and close for the leader or the step and cross for the follower are danced Quick, Quick &. I have not added an interval of time here but rather designated a split between the rise and fall. Alternatively the figure may be danced Slow, Slow, Slow, Slow &. The idea of splitting the rise from the fall is the same. This timing will need greater body control using the slow rhythm during the crossing action and rise and fall.

La Salida: As an Entrance to The Dance Floor:

When teaching I describe la Salida as the action of stepping sideways to invite the lady out on to the dance floor, thus outlet.
I have already dealt with the issue of a backward start. For purposes of review it can be bothersome to new dancers of Argentine Tango. There are two major reasons and some solutions that I will deal with. The First is the inherent jeopardy of backing against line of dance. The Second is struggling with the idea (physically & mentally) of beginning with the leader's right foot to begin a dance.

Entering the dance floor can always be a problem once the music has started and the dancers have begun moving so obviously it is

Follower's never loose control of your body during any lowering action from a crossed position!

Step #4 Walk To The Cross Lady's Cross and Man's Close

79

preferable to be on the dance floor in a ready position between Tangos. Then you may start with the left foot to the side for your Salida which of course may become coincidental with the first step of The Walk to The Cross. Or a leader's Stroll forward in either crossed or parallel feet. The forward walk assumes you are not within two dance strides of another couple.

The leader begins with a flex into the supporting leg through the knee bringing the follower into the music and both move away from that knee with the compression of the thigh. This will work in any dance that has a knee flex as part of its supporting leg characteristic!

More often than not you will have to enter the floor after things have begun. Do so from the corner of the floor, as opposed to along the line of dance, because couples are changing to the new line of dance here and inherently are the most cautious. This will give you the opportunity to accelerate onto the floor just after a moving couple has passed you. According to your level of experience with the partner at hand it may be wisest just to Stroll onto the floor to physically feel the intensity of the music together.

The leader must remember and prepare his partner when beginning a dance:

The leader must be sure that he has his partner securely on her left foot before beginning. I like to start on the balls of both feet as if I had already been dancing and create the proper inclination of my body to assure the good start.

Step #1 of The Tango Close (el Resolucion)

The Tango Close (el Resolucion)

This is the most common transitional figure and a great contributor to the character of the dance. Remember Tango is a conversation with pauses from one topic or mood to the next.

1. Start with a Tango Walk forward for the leader and backward for the follower. Do not forget that you are doing Argentine Tango. Walk with good tone through the feet and big toes while maintaining contact with the floor.

2. The second step is to the side with the free foot of both partners. Make the contact of this side step with the inside edge (closest to

80

your center) of the toe and ball of the foot while releasing from the standing foot in the same way. This will give you very smooth release from and entry into the feet. The width of this side step must not be wider than the width of your hips. If this step is taken from a Right Outside Partner Position it may be necessary for the leader to stride slightly wider to consummate in line with the partner.

3. For the third step, to make el Resolucion a successful transitional figure we close to the balls of both feet. You will move to a slight rise with no heel contact along with a very controlled bracing action of the knees. This will enable you to create transition to either foot for the choice of the following figure. To create the lead for the choice of the next foot, the gentleman will use his good frame and connection with his partner. He will slightly incline the entirety of his spinal column (the Atlas Axis joint through the coccyx bone) away from the foot he desires to release, thus creating a new standing foot.

**Step #2 of The Tango Close
(el Resolucion)
Man's Right foot to the side**

Followers, please do not make the mistake of guessing or assuming which foot is next! A better idea is to wait for the lead at the top of the slight rise and then practice good foot and leg speed towards the next position without sacrificing your balance or frame. This action in Argentine Tango is what I would describe as a life skill; over the life of your dancing you will get better and better at it. You will eventually get to the point where the transition is hardly visible so please do not get discouraged while learning.

Once you have learned this figure it may be wise to start the dance on the balls of both feet. Then incline your frame in place to create the standing foot. In this way you may use various starts contingent on available floor space and the desired figure. I like it because it brings us into the music with cat-like composure.

A note to teachers and students of the Ballroom style Tango: If you compare this step to it's Ballroom counterpart (The Tango Draw) new students of the Argentine Tango will use more mental imaging than you want. Heel leads will occur on the forward walk and you will get a Tango Draw without a weight change on the third step.

**Step #3 of The Tango Close
(el Resolucion)
Man standing on Right foot
preparing to close**

Timing: I always attempt to dance el Resolucion as Quick, Quick, Slow. My belief is this truly amplifies the end of the present topic of conversation. If the music's cadenza (tempo) was moving briskly and did suggest a stop or pause I would be inclined to use el Resolucion as a connecting figure and in this case would dance it Quick, Quick, Quick &.

The Eight Patterns (El Ocho)

Man prepares to lead Lady's Forward Ocho

The Spanish name for the number 8 is Ocho. The figure derives its name from the shape of the dancer's movement that very closely resembles the shape of an 8. Let us define the content of a physical Ocho as a dance movement. In its simplest form the Ocho is a pivot of 180° done by the follower after a weight change that evolves naturally as a result of a change of body direction transmitted through the frame of the leader. An ocho is a figure type that does not mirror the partner's image. The leader can actually be stationary with feet together or apart. The leader can also do la Cunita (the rock) with the collecting action of the foot or holding the foot in CBMP. In a more advanced form the leader can self impose similar movements of rotation, but at this early stage this is not our focus.

Ochos can evolve from preceding steps in any direction and can rotate forward or backward into the turn. They are done easily in front of or in an outside partner position. The ochos are obedient to the following rules: Step Then Turn, The Rule of Torque, The Tandem Usage of The Body (shoulder to ribs and ribs to hips) for leading and following rotation. Please review these rules and exercises.

Lady's Forward Ocho with Adornment

As I have stated, an Ocho will start in one direction and rotate 180° after the weight change has been made, to finish in the opposite direction. Following the rule of torque, the leader can easily cause the follower to rotate to the new direction once she has achieved a new vertical center. This is the key to a successful rotation in any form of partner dancing! The leader's responsibility is to wait until the shoulders, ribs, and hips of his partner are parallel and in line, then lead the Ocho.

The partner that is leading (in a more advanced form either can lead figures in the dance) the Ocho requires good solid contact with the floor throughout the periphery of his shoes. The leader also needs a good solid base along with a balanced and controlled frame. The leader can rock to a weight change with his partner on the outside (right side of the leader's frame). The leader can change from forward to backward directions with a rock (replacement step) while bracing the knees then accelerate by administering a feeling of both rotation and pressure into the floor. It is imperative to leave the lady's ribs, hips, and shoulders parallel to the dance floor as well as parallel to the gentleman's frame. He leads with strong CBM and torque within his body's center. His frame follows and transfers the rotation to his partner. She will get more rotation than he by virtue of being on the outside of the curve.

82

The leader waits until his partner has achieved both impact, structure, and the beginning of compression (see: "Dynamic Duo") before administering the gestures of a figure 8 through his wrists and elbows. This leading of rotation requires much practice! You must develop the sensitivity to feel the compressive movement in the follower's knees which will be transmitted through her frame. If there is bullish power or static tension in the joints of either partner the transmission of the "Dynamic Duo," will be hidden or lost. When dancing focus and use the center of your muscles rather than the tiny extensors and flexors around the joints. This will help avoid the stiff unnatural feeling and appearance.

Man and Lady finish forward Ocho in CBMP

The leader should not break his frame by relaxing the underarms thus leaving the upper arms uninvolved. Rather he uses his entire arm in conjunction with the body itself along with breathing (flexing) primarily at the elbows and wrists. Once again I need to remind you before we begin the Ocho, it is **not** an application of strength or power. A strong frame internalizes your power and administers it only as the follower needs. Simply stated, the follower determines what she needs, not the leader! Therefore geometric accuracy of direction and directional leads becomes incredibly important!

The above statement was my basis for writing Quickstart To Social Dancing. Geometric accuracy is simple, yet frequently ignored. An error in direction by the leader is amplified by the follower. Once the lead has been administered the follower takes on the role of the leader until the figure is resolved. When teaching a couple I say, "Show her where to go and then follow her there!"

Conclude the Ocho's rotation with a flex in the knees by the leader that will be transmitted to the follower. Please on behalf of followers everywhere do not try to stop rotation abruptly with your hands alone! This is like hanging up the phone before the conversation is done.

The Leg Action for Ocho and Grapevine Figures:

Balance and Timing are the key ingredients of successful dancing at any level! The leading and following of Ochos and Grapevines are a test of your development of these skills. The proper dispersal of the follower's body weight must include support on the commencing foot, between the feet, and on the concluding foot. There can be no moments of unsupported movement or rotation while at the same time retaining the character of the dance!   As a general rule, as the knees separate they straighten and as they converge they flex.

An Argentine Tango Walk includes the collection of the knees as a walk concludes or as the direction of the body changes.   Therefore the knees will collect under the corresponding pelvis and gain contact with each other through the actual turn of any Ocho or Grapevine.   Elevation or rise is responsive to speed and quantity of rotation.

As the speed of the ocho or grapevine action is increased the knees will straighten.   As the degree of rotation increases or as rotation increases with speed, the knees will straighten. Therefore a slowing, hesitating, or stopping action can be created for the purposes of changing direction or for the development of any or a series of Adornments by flexing or remaining flexed in the knees.   You will also find that the elevation changes of the feet work harmoniously and in conjunction with the knees.

Defining the transaction of leading and following

Questions always arrive about whether to cross or not to cross and if so in which direction? First, here is my definition of leading.   I firmly believe that first the body of the leader transmits directional or rotational lead.   The leader's arms and hands must then be a secondary response to his own body. This quantitative lead is then transmitted responsibly (so as not to negatively challenge the follower's balance) through the couple's connection (shoulders, arms & hands) to the follower's body.   So the leader's body creates a desired degree of rotation or linear progression with either acceleration or deceleration.   To these factors the follower's body would then reciprocate.   The follower, in essence becomes the leader by creating space, for her partner to fill, allowing him to start this process again.   Therefore countless leads and follows occur through the course of a dance.   As more of this activity occurs the quantity of each lead becomes more subtle and done with more finesse.   The result is a highly skilled and very smooth dance couple.

To address the issue of crossing or no crossing legs of I have had to include this definition. Having done so, the follower's pelvis is in a position at the time of the passage of the knees that is either in a level plane with, or has created an angle from her supporting side. If the plane is level at the knees passage, you may step forward, backward, side with progression, or close if there is no progression. If there is an angle at the time of passage then some degree of rotation has occurred.   An imaginary tangent will project perpendicularly through the front and rear of the unsupported pelvis. The dancer must step in line with this tangent or she will be fighting the direction of her own body and its momentum.

84

In addition to speed (fast or slow) on a close, cross, or adornment, the actual action of the moving leg must in no way contribute to any loss of balance or inadvertent body movement in oneself or your partner!!

Here is a last word of caution regarding the knees and the ankles. Good dancers straighten and release both the knees and the ankles through the usage of the center of the large muscles of the legs. To that I would add, never create rise or fall, or any action that contains a basic plié (bending of the knees) or relevé (lifting of the body onto the balls of the feet) by initiating these movements from the joints. As I mentioned above the extensors and flexors surrounding the joints should not bear the load, it will result in stiff, stilted, or robotic movement.

Styling preferences for the free leg of the Ocho include skimming the floor with the toe, and lifting and maintaining the shin in a parallel position to the floor. These two are the most basic, but please do not limit yourself. You may developed your own adorning movements.

The conclusion of either of the above includes leaving the toe under the corresponding pelvis or placing the foot in CBMP. I recommend that you vary your Ochos. One note of caution, at the conclusion of the 180° rotation the follower should put her free foot down if she maintains the elevated style before she passes to the next movement. A flex in the standing leg is also required here to give you smooth entry to the next step.

Timing: There are seemingly unlimited varieties according to la cadencia of the music and the skill of the couple. Some of these are Slow Ochos, Quick Ochos, or even double time (half beat) Ochos.

In all of the Argentine Tango patterns the Leader's movement will be described first, with the follower's movement in parenthesis. Please remember these patterns are only suggested forms to incorporate the figures we have been discussing. The essence of this dance is improvisation that always takes into account good physical logic and the physical philosophy we are working towards.

Simple Pattern including the Forward Ochos:

1. Left Foot Stroll forward in Parallel Feet: (the natural opposite)
   Timing: Slow

2. Right Foot Stroll forward in Parallel Feet: (the natural opposite)
   Timing: Slow

3. The Walk to The Cross: Steps 1 - 4 Left, Right, Left, Right (the natural opposite)   Timing: Slow, Slow, Quick, Quick

4. Left Foot Stroll forward in Parallel Feet: (the natural opposite)
   Timing: Slow

5. Right Foot Stroll forward in Parallel Feet: (the natural opposite)
   Timing: Slow

6. La Cunita: Left foot forward, prepare to Rock by flexing knees at the moment of collection (the natural opposite)   Timing: Quick

7. La Cunita: Right foot backward to conclude the 2nd step of the Rock (the natural opposite)   Timing: Quick

8. The Follower's Forward Ocho Clockwise: The Left foot backward holding the Right foot in CBMP and leading a clockwise forward Ocho with the frame, please review Ocho technique. End with flex in the Left knee. (Right foot forward Ocho turning 180° clockwise collecting the left foot and then end with the left foot in CBMP to match the leader's leg line) This is the first half of the 8. Timing: Slow

9. The Follower's Forward Ocho Counterclockwise: The Right foot forward collecting the Left foot and leading a counterclockwise forward Ocho with the frame. End with flex in the Right knee. (Left foot forward Ocho turning 180° counterclockwise end by collecting the Right knee) This is the second half of the 8. Timing: Slow

10. Both repeat Step Number Nine (9) Timing: Slow

11. Both repeat Step Number Ten (10) Timing: Slow

12. The Tango Close (el Resolucion): Left foot forward (The Natural Opposite) Please review the technique of el Resolucion. Timing: Quick

13. The Tango Close (el Resolucion) Right foot to the side slightly wider than a normal width (Left foot to the side the width of the torso.   Timing: Quick

14. The Tango Close (el Resolucion) Close Left foot to right foot with weight on balls of both feet and experience very slight rise. (The natural opposite)   Timing: Slow

15. Both repeat steps numbered 6 through 15 having led the follower to their left foot leaving their right foot free of body weight.

The Grapevine:

This is a **linear developmental figure** in the Argentine Tango that travels along the line of dance. This figure is being presented in this text so that the philosophical logic, relating to the Giros, will be understood and then doable.   Because this figure would travels so quickly down line of dance you will seldom if ever, use it in a congested social setting!

You are better off to think of this figure as a preliminary development of the following patterns known as Giros (Turns).   If you should dance the Grapevine please restrict it to one pattern of four steps. We do need to develop the Grapevine action since it will become a major portion of your Argentine Tango.   You should be made aware that the physical attitude of the follower is to Stroll backward at all times and the changes of direction are felt and lead through the leader's frame.   Therefore the Grapevine is a development of the leader and not to be taken for granted by the follower.   In this way the use and pleasures of layering **Adornments** to your Tango will be a function of mutual cooperation.

**Side Step to lady's left foot
1st Step of the Grapevine**

The legs must be thought of as one of two vine components. The main vine is the directional vine and always travels sideways from the position of the former foot.   That is to say, if the body is traveling left or counter-clockwise, the left foot is the main vine.   The secondary vine weaves. This would make the right foot the weaving vine starting either crossing forward or back.   To maintain lead of the crossing action the leader must brace or flex the knees more as they converge and pass and then straighten as they separate. This is due to inherent rise produced as the knees converge giving the dancer a feeling of lift.   The lead is maintained by a toned frame with arms parallel to the dance floor breathing through the elbows and wrists.   The arms must move in tandem with the direction of the ribs and hips while maintaining the good frame. The follower will feel acceleration, cross, and rotation in tandem with their leader.   Please review the technique above regarding closing and crossing the legs.

Between each weight change there is a rotation of no more than 45° toward and then away from the direction of the main vine (directional side step).   The characteristic of the Argentine Tango Walk must be observed in that knees pass under the corresponding pelvis.   As the knees pass, the pivot will occur.   While developing your skill in this movement, as a leader it would be wise to observe the passage of the follower's knees before attempting the lead to the 45° rotation. Please review Rotation in Tango.   Additionally I have found that this figure and the Giro (further ahead in this text) are resolved best by

**Lady crosses right foot behind
left foot
2nd Step of the Grapevine**

students when the leader increases the floor pressure of both the supporting foot and the tone of the moving foot. This will create what is known as a delayed walk in dancing. The very slight delaying action will insure that the follower's **Grapevine** is creamy and smooth.

A complete pattern would be four weight changes. Beginners should do them in opposition with their partner. That is, the action of a forward cross would be reciprocated by a back cross. Alternately we would have a side step and a cross or a cross, and then a side step, based on the preceding figure and the entry point of the Grapevine.

Simple Pattern including the Grapevine and the Back Ochos:

Start by having curved a Tango Close to face the outside of the dance floor (facing wall). You may also Stroll to face the wall or start at a corner backing diagonally to the center of the floor. You may substitute the following timings to all Slow rhythm.

1. Step Sideways: with Left foot facing the wall. Commence to turn Counterclockwise. (The Natural Opposite) Timing: Quick
   Step numbers 1 and 2 are an example of overlapping one figure with another. This is a common trait of Tango and will become a very useful transitional device.

2. The Grapevine: Right foot crosses in front of Left. Commence to turn Clockwise. (The Natural Opposite) Timing: Quick

3. The Grapevine: Left foot to the side. Commence to turn Counterclockwise. (The Natural Opposite) Timing: Quick

4. The Grapevine: Right foot crosses behind Left. Commence to turn Clockwise. (The Natural Opposite) Timing: Quick

5. The Grapevine: Left foot to the side preparing to step Right Outside Partner. (Right foot to the side) Timing: Quick

6. The Follower's Back Ocho Clockwise: The Right foot forward and collecting the Left, lead a clockwise Back Ocho with the frame, please review Ocho technique. End with flex in the Right knee. (Left foot Back Ocho turning 180° clockwise collecting the Right foot) This is the first half of the 8. Timing: Slow

7. The Follower's Back Ocho Counterclockwise: The Left foot backward and collecting the Right foot and leading a Counterclockwise Back Ocho with the frame. End with flex in the Left knee. (Right foot Back Ocho turning 180° counterclockwise

collecting the left foot)This is the second half of the 8.
Timing: Slow

8. Right Foot Forward Stroll: Right Foot forward in Right Outside Partner Position (Left foot back collecting the Right foot)
Timing: Slow

9. The Tango Close (el Resolucion): Left foot forward (The Natural Opposite) Please review the technique of el Resolucion.
Timing: Quick

10. The Tango Close (el Resolucion) Right foot to the side slightly wider than a normal width (Left foot to the side the width of the torso.
Timing: Quick

11. The Tango Close (el Resolucion) Close Left foot to right foot with weight on balls of both feet and experience very slight rise. (The natural opposite)
Timing: Slow

Ocho action to change directions of vine during a Giro

Giro (The Grapevine Turning):

The word Giro simply means turn is Spanish. For the couple as a whole it refers to the turning movement or pivoting clockwise or counterclockwise. In the **social** Argentine Tango the couple does not break from their dance frame. This is the reason there are no underarm turns for either the man or the women. Teachers and students of this social dance therefore refer to the turning Grapevine as a Giro. Another common name for this figure is el **Molinete** (Toy windmill). Its grapevine action by one member of the couple around the other takes on the appearance of the horse or oxen that turn the hub of an old grinding mill. One problem with the usage of the word Molinete is that another more advanced but popular figure is called a **Calisita (Merry-Go-Round)**. This figure is developed by the man walking the lady around while she is supported on only one foot. The fact that both words, Calisita and Molinete, reflect such a similar usage we will just use the term **Giro**.

Our example (beginner level) will have the follower traveling in the areas between the outermost circumference and the hub (the leader himself and the couple's frames become the radius). This of course suggests that the leader may also do the vine action around the follower but leave that for next week! Giros may travel in either a clockwise or counterclockwise rotation. We will also change directions by using the ochos. This figure is wonderful fun!
The leader will use the action of **Enrosque** to enter the Giro or **Turning Grapevine** and exit while completing an ocho.

Lady's left leg in front of right to begin Giro counterclockwise

Man's Chair (La Sentada)

Enrosque (To Twist or Screw In): is the action of an in place foot swivel to complete enough rotation to end facing your partner. The leader will be on the inside of the curve while his partner is on the outside of the curve thus giving the partners to rotate at varying intervals. The twist must be initiated from the leader's center using the outside or free side of their body and the free leg's thigh in tandem to create the necessary speed of rotation. No inadvertent or residual effect can be experienced by the partner or the dance police will be alerted immediately! Therefore the dancer must practice this technique alone prior to exposing your partner to your Enrosque.

Once the Giro has been initiated, the leader may continue with Enrosque technique or change to, heel to instep footwork which would be a form of a Chassé. The leader must develop the sensitivity to be able to determine, at any time, which foot their partner is on to provide a clear exit from the Giro.

An illustration that has served me well through my teaching career for this type of figure since a form of it can be done in virtually every dance is as follows: There is a circular garden located at the center of your lawn with an edging approximately 3 inches above the garden. The radius of the garden is approximately 18 inches +/-. The leader faces the periphery of the garden from its center and the follower stands on the edging and cannot enter the garden. Take your framing position and proceed with a clockwise or counterclockwise Grapevine. Your arms must breath according to the formerly described technique. The follower will use foot swivel as the knees pass in relevé (lifting of the body onto the balls of the feet) while continually adjusting the facing position of the garden's center. There you have it a Giro!

The Chair (La Sentada)

This figure is an attractive pose that resembles the silhouette of a chair. It can be done by either partner singularly or alternatively. La Sentada falls within the category of a Corté (stopping or pausing action). It is led with a wider step than the Cunita (Rock) The leader rocks to a wider than normal stance and places the area of the Achilles Tendon just above the kneecap of the flexed supporting leg. Beginners can be aided in initiating this figure by the leader's very gentle contact using their upper thigh of the new supporting leg. The leader will place their thigh just a smidgen under the thigh of the follower. Strong bracing through the knees is required with a graduating weight change between the feet rather than all at once. This means you will finish the leg line at the moment of the completed compression. The leader may further delay la Sentada by remaining braced in the knees. I should make note that I have described the strictly social version of la Sentada. There is also a host of stage or performance level versions of this figure where one partner actually sits in the other's lap.

Simple Pattern including Giro, La Sentada, Enrosque and Ochos:

1. The Salida to Finish in Right Outside Partner Position: Both do the first two steps of la Salida   Timing: Slow, Slow

2. La Sentada: Using the former technique the leader will take his Sentada by stepping back on the Left foot (Right foot forward) Timing: Slow

3. La Sentada: Using the former technique the leader will step forward on the Right Foot. (The follower will step back and achieve la Sentada)   Timing: Slow

4. Follower's Forward Clockwise Ocho with Leader's Enrosque: The leader will develop a Forward Clockwise Ocho for the follower by stepping back on the left foot. First leading the Ocho then snapping into an Enrosque in a clockwise direction. The leader will remain on their left foot throughout with feet now together (Right foot 1/2 inch from the floor) having placed himself at the hub of the Giro. The leader must maintain a small degree of flex in the knees preparing to lead the first side movement. (Follower's Forward Clockwise Ocho on the Right foot) Timing: Slow

Lady's Chair (la Sentada)

5. Giro Clockwise by the follower while the leader either continues with Enrosque or heel to instep Chassé: Leader remains in place rotating clockwise (Side Left foot)   Timing: Quick

6. Giro Clockwise: Leader remains in place rotating clockwise with Enrosque or heel to instep Chassé (Right foot crosses behind) Timing: Quick

7. Giro Clockwise: Leader remains in place rotating clockwise with Enrosque or heel to instep Chassé (Left foot to side) Timing: Quick

8. Giro Clockwise to Forward Ocho Action: Leader remains in place rotating clockwise with Enrosque or heel to instep Chassé preparing to lead a Forward Clockwise Ocho (Right foot cross in front to Ocho action clockwise)   Timing: Quick

9. Giro Counterclockwise: Leader remains in place rotating counterclockwise with Enrosque or heel to instep Chassé (Left foot crosses in front)   Timing: Quick

10. Giro Counterclockwise: Leader remains in place rotating counterclockwise with Enrosque or heel to instep Chassé (Right foot side)   Timing: Quick

11. Giro Counterclockwise: Leader remains in place rotating counterclockwise with Enrosque or heel to instep Chassé (Left foot crosses behind)   Timing: Quick

12. Giro Counterclockwise: Leader remains in place rotating counterclockwise with Enrosque or heel to instep Chassé (Right foot to the side)   Timing: Quick

13. Giro Counterclockwise: Leader remains in place rotating counterclockwise with Enrosque or heel to instep Chassé and preparing to lead Forward Counterclockwise Ocho to finish facing each other. **The leader will end with weight on their Right foot.** (Left foot crosses in front with Ocho action to finish facing partner)   Timing: Slow

14. El Resolucion: Both do three steps of the El Resolucion. Timing: Quick, Quick, Slow.

Notes for above: The terming of *Ocho Action* is used to denote a rotation of less than 180°, according to the leader's rotation, facing position on the dance floor, and skill. While rehearsing this pattern the couple may substitute Steps 5 through 12 with all Slow count timing.

Adornments (el Adornos):

Improvisation is a key ingredient to the Tango. As I have mentioned earlier in the text a Tango dance is a conversation between partners. Conversations have moods and topics and herein lies the ability to actually make the dance the theater of improvisation. We can be angry with our lover and try to create provocation as we dance. Our mood can be one of enticement, allure, invitation, and sensuality. The portrayal of these ideas are not new or unique to dancing through the use of various dance positions with the arms and body. The fact that the social Tango does so with the feet and legs without the release of framing position make it unique to the world of dance. Since the early 1980's it has become fashionable for the women of Tango to accessorize or adorn the dance developing their conversation with their partner. During the Golden Age of Tango this action of adornment would have belonged to the man as a demonstration of masculinity and bravado. It would have been a women of less than genteel character who would have adorned through the dance in other than the most basic movements. Today the ability of a women's Tango is measured by what would have had her dismissed from any polite company.

These **adornments** are pauses or stops in the conversation to heighten or accent our expression. They are done so by bracing the knee with the supporting at varying elevations so as to manipulate the free leg as follows: Off the floor, on the floor, on yourself or your partner, or between your partner's legs.   I have not included adornments in our patterns because that would be contrived. You must experience them for yourselves. Do so between any figure type described in this section of the text including just a single Stroll (Tango walk) if you wish. Adornments are like accessorizing after you have put on the main wardrobe. The technique of delaying the leader or the follower includes bracing with supporting knee at the time of the collection under the pelvis and adorning from a secure position.

Here are some examples of simple adornments:

Adornment
Lady's Shoeshine

Toe Taps (el Golpes): Simple tapping of the inside edge or ball of the sole of the shoe. It is not considered good social form to actually make noise with your feet as is the case with Flamenco dancing.   The Adornment is used strictly for visual and musical interpretation. The stomping of feet should be reserved for the stage or performance level of Tango. El Zapateado would be an example of this.

Pencil (El Lápiz) This is the act of drawing circles on the floor at or around your own or your partner's feet with the toe or inside edge of your free foot.   They are strictly improvisational and are used to create response either your partner or onlookers. El Lápiz often accompanies the back side front steps of your partner's grapevine during a Giro.   While moving the free leg or foot, be careful not to cause loss of balance. This is not one of the desired responses!

Adornment
Man's Shoeshine

**Adornment
Lady's Boleo**

The Boleo:

Is an Adornment applied to the follower that is fully created and developed by the leader in terms of quantity and speed. The follower therefore resolves the Boleo only to the extent of their form of foot or leg action. The leader creates an **in and out twist** or change of direction with the partner's frame. The follower's choice then is to have one or both legs fully extended. The most popular variety includes one legged support so as to feel full stretch behind that legs knee with shin of the free leg at right angle to the standing leg. The knees and thighs should be in firm contact with each other. Another example of the Boleo would be to twist with the instep of the free foot crossed and pressed behind the ankle of the standing leg. The leader develops the Boleo from a linear movement such as a stroll or side step and uses the rock step or remains stationary while twisting their partner in their entirety from a normal frame. This twist includes the standing foot position. At times this figure can be called an **Amague** similar to a fake or change of direction in soccer. The most important point of the Boleo is the exit that occurs within the leader's resolve of the music and not of the follower's. A flex in the leader's knee and a movement to CBMP (See: Rotation) will effectively end the partner's resolve of the Boleo to the leader's timing. The trick here is to develop the sensitivity to changes of elevation and direction of the leader's frame and not to anticipate the Boleo.

Congratulations, we have concluded the over 30 step variations in the style of Argentine Tango. The use of this text will amply prepare you to dance an Argentine Tango at any social occasion. The technique in general and specific to the Argentine Tango will take the reader well beyond the choreographical bounds presented in Quickstart To Tango. As mentioned previously there are virtually unlimited varieties of Tango patterns available for your usage and pleasure. I recommend that you use this text as a personal Tango notebook and outline and then find a competent instructor in your area to continue your development of the Argentine Tango. **Tango On!**

Your Notes:

American Tango:

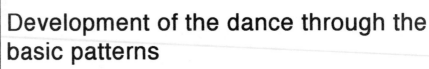

The Choreography and Its Technique

We will develop your choreography in a cumulative fashion. In the following step patterns I will describe the foot positions numerically. We will then take each of the numbered foot positions and amplify our discussion of how to do it. The notes will appear separately so that your charts will become an easy visual reference. We will frequently refer to your Quickstart exercises where there is overlapping technique and will amplify any new material for your benefit. Once you have executed each numbered foot position several times you will find it unnecessary to refer to the general description over and over again. This will allow you to learn additional figures, otherwise known as step patterns, quickly.

American Tango Man's Left Forward Walk

Development of the dance through the basic patterns

The Basic Patterns

The content of the basic step in tango is really three separate dance figures. These separate dance figures will include varied positions and components, amounts of turn or curve, and what we could call "tango atmosphere." The Basic Tango patterns really contain the essence of the tango.

American Tango Man's Right Forward Walk

Understanding the tango basic construction will provide us with virtually all of the characteristics that define what tango is, how it is to be danced, how it is felt. I must make an important note before you begin the following choreography: line of dance or LOD must be observed at all times when dancing in public. LOD is a term for the counter-clockwise traveling pattern in the ballroom while dancing Tango. When you first start dancing in public it may be wise to contain your dancing to the outermost periphery of the dance floor available to you. As you gain confidence start to move in diagonal tangents from the edges of the floor to the center of the floor and back to the outer circumference of the dance floor. Think of a herring bone pattern or zigzag line traveling counter-clockwise around the dance floor. If you fail to adhere to this LOD it is likely that you will become a nuisance to other dancers, and you should expect a call from the Dance Police!

Timing of the basic figures 1 through 5:

The following four figures all have the same timing using eight beats of music: Slow (1,2); Slow (3,4); Quick (5); Quick (6); Slow (7,8). I recommend that you employ the verbalization of the spelling of the word TANGO (T,A,N,G,O) that we discussed earlier in the text. This will certainly make your initial experience with the choreography a lot of fun!

The drama is ready to unfold. Are you ready for your exploration of the Tango? The following figures will take you from one smoldering or sensual location on the dance floor to the next. These figures will move you from troubled congestion, to a special place where you and your partner can be alone with your Tango. Alone with your passions, and yet you've traveled to a place where all can see.

Man in place on right foot preparing to draw

Pattern 1) The Forward Basic Figure (can be used without or with curve) :

| Step No. 1: | The gentleman will step forward on his **left** foot. The lady will step backwards on her **right** foot. |

Step No. 1:   The gentleman will step forward on his **left** foot.
The lady will step backwards on her **right** foot.

Step No. 2:   The gentleman will step forward on his **right** foot.
The lady will step backwards on her **left** foot.

Step No. 3   The gentleman will step forward on his **left** foot.
The lady will step backwards on per **right** foot.

Step No. 4   The gentlemen will step side on his **right** foot.
The lady will step side on her **left** foot.

Step No. 5   The gentleman will draw his **left** foot towards his right foot without a weight change.
The lady will draw her **right** foot towards her left foot without a weight change.

The Tango Draw

Man's Left foot forward in Promenade Position

Pattern 2) The Backward Basic Figure (can be used without or with curve):

Step No. 1:	The gentleman will step backwards on his **left** foot. The lady will step forward on her **right** foot.
Step No. 2:	The gentleman will step backwards on his **right** foot. The lady will step forward on her **left** foot.
Step No. 3	The gentleman will step backwards on his **left** foot. The lady will step forward on her **right** foot.
Step No. 4	The gentlemen will step side on his **right** foot. The lady will step side on her **left** foot.
Step No. 5	The gentleman will draw his **left** foot towards his right foot without a weight change. The lady will draw her **right** foot towards her **left** foot without a weight change.

Man's right foot forward and across in PP and CBMP

Pattern 3) The Promenade Basic Figure With Left Turn:

Please note: the following promenade figures may curve as well as turn.

Step No. 1:	The gentleman will step forward in PP (promenade position) on his **left** foot. The lady will step forward in PP (promenade position) on her **right** foot.
Step No. 2:	The gentleman will step forward and across in PP on his **right** foot. The lady will step forward and across in PP on her **left** foot.
Step No. 3	The gentleman will step forward in PP on his **left** foot and then turn 1/4 to the left leading the lady to face him in the basic closed position.

The lady will step forward in PP on her right foot and then turn 1/4 to the left to finish backing in the basic closed position.

Step No. 4

The gentlemen will step side on his right foot.
The lady will step side on her left foot.

Step No. 5

The gentleman will draw his left foot towards his right foot without a weight change.
The lady will draw her right foot towards her left foot without a weight change.

Pattern 4) The Promenade Basic Figure With Right Turn:

Step No. 1:

The gentleman will step forward in PP (promenade position) on his left foot.
The lady will step forward in PP (promenade position) on her right foot.

Step No. 2:

The gentleman will step forward and across in PP on his right foot and then turn 1/4 to the right leading the lady to face him in the basic closed position.
The lady will step forward and across in PP on her left foot and then turn 1/4 to the right to finish backing in the basic closed position.

Step No. 3

The gentleman will step side on his left foot.
The lady will step side on her right foot.

Step No. 4

The gentleman will replace his weight onto his right foot (The right foot was still in the position of step #2).
The lady will replace her weight onto her left foot (The left foot was still in the position of step #2).

Step No. 5

The gentleman will draw his left foot towards his right foot without a weight change.
The lady will draw her right foot towards her left foot without a weight change.

The development and description of each Step Number from The Basic Patterns One through Five in the Ballroom Tango

Step No's. 1 & 2: Employ the techniques you have developed in the stalking walk exercises. You have learned that each and every forward or backward step may curve. To develop the ability to curve, you will have to use CBM and CBMP on each step number one. The gentleman will employ right shoulder leading (the lady uses left shoulder leads) on step number two. Please remember that there is no rise and fall in American Tango. The use of knee veer and sighting a line on the wall will assist you in preventing rise. Rework the stalking walk exercise with your partner as you develop these figures. Do each figure with and without contact using the necessary techniques. Remember that you develop physical skills through physical action, movement, and touch. My words will become more meaningful as you practice. In the above descriptions I have indicated that a curve may be used in Step numbers 1 and 2. Actually this is my preference. In this way you best experience the feeling, the atmosphere, of the tango you developed in your curving exercises! Experiment with greater or lesser degrees of turn or curve to create patterns to circle the ballroom. I like to have fun by dancing one or two basic Tango figures with a moderate curve followed by a basic figure with a very tight curve all the way around the room. By being able to do this the couple will demonstrate their prowess in balance, control, and floorcraft.

I want to give you an example of what experimentation with your basic Tango figures can lead to. We will use the example of figure No. 2. In its simplest form this figure will begin backing and end backing. I want to demonstrate to you the potential of changing a simple figure to a rather exciting basic figure. Hopefully, you will continue to experiment with the components of each basic amalgamation. Remember that the tango basic is really three separate figures. They consist of two walks either forward, backwards, or in promenade position (PP), and the Tango draw.

In Step No. 2 the following description was given: "The gentleman will step forward and across in PP on his **right** foot." This means he will move his right leg in the direction of promenade position and promenade direction (This means the couple is traveling together in the same direction). To accomplish this the gentleman must release his right foot from the dance floor and step over his left foot by the smallest of margins. This is done so that the couple can retain control in their direction without inadvertently bumping each other's position.

100

The following illustrates how a basic figure can become a unique variation. This than will become step pattern No. 5.

Pattern 5) A variation of the backward basic figure with curve to finish forward or in PP:

Step No. 1:   The gentleman will step backwards on his left foot with his left shoulder leading with slight curve left.
The lady will step forward on her right foot with her right shoulder leading with slight curve left.

Step No. 2:   The gentleman will step backwards on his right foot in CBMP and using CBM. He will curve a total of a quarter turn (90 degrees) on steps number 1 & 2 if PP is desired, or curve an additional quarter turn to the left on steps numbers 3 & 4 if the basic position is to be used for the following figure.
The lady will step forward on her left foot and follow the curving action her partner develops.

Step No. 3   The gentleman will step forward on his left foot from the position of step 2 if PP is desired, or step diagonally forward if the basic position is to be used for the following figure.
The lady will either step backward from the position of step 2 or diagonally backward on her right foot based on her partner's body position.

Step No. 4   The gentleman will step side on his right foot.
The lady will step side on her left foot.

Step No. 5   The gentleman will draw his left foot towards his right foot without a weight change in either basic or PP. This will be based on the overall curve he has created and the direction he wishes to take next.
The lady will draw her right foot towards her left foot without a weight change to finish in either PP or basic position.

It is my hope that by interpreting and developing pattern No. 5 you will see the unlimited potential for varying each basic step in the Tango. Do this by using varying amounts of curve to produce an infinite variety of step patterns and directions.

As we continue to demonstrate additional figures in this text you will find that there are infinite ways to vary each of them. Each new figure pattern may be influenced greatly or gently by the use of curve.

The Tango Draw — In Depth

The last segment of the basic step in the American tango is known as the Tango Draw. These are Step Numbers 3, 4, & 5. This Step pattern will be repeated several times in Quickstart To Tango. The Tango draw can be used either as a connecting (known as a linking figure) and as a concluding figure to the great majority of dance patterns in the American Tango.

It is imperative that you do this figure well! Therefore we will spend a good deal of time with it. Let's begin.

The importance of Step No. 4 is often overlooked in the Tango Draw. Beginners, in their attempts to do the side step that follows, will rush and leave this forward step unfinished. Because Step No. 4 is done to the count of a quick, or one beat of music, they do not develop a full weight change and thus do not create a good vertical axis on which to rotate or change direction. Both the partners will have the opportunity to step forward with either the forward Tango Draw (man) or the backward Tango Draw (lady), so help one another here. Make sure when you do this step, particularly when going forward or in PP, your knee is over your toes and your hips are over your knee. The control of the abdominal wall will insure that your spinal column will remain completely vertical, that is to say perpendicular to the dance floor, and as a result shoulders will remain over your hips. We dealt with these physical issues in the Tango exercises. Your ability to rotate, curve, and lead or follow additional figures will be stymied if this Step No. 4 is not taken properly. This step may be taken with or without CBMP, depending on whether or not rotation is desired.

Step No. 5: This is generally a side step and therefore should be taken with contact on the inside edge of your foot so the body has a chance to roll smoothly and quickly over the foot. This side step can be improved by placing the foot slightly forward of the plane of Step Number 4. Slightly forward (slightly back if you are the lady) would be measured as a position of the foot in which the foot taking the side step would be advanced 2 to 3 inches from the position of the standing leg and then taken side. This will enhance your ability to rotate especially to create the lead or follow to promenade position. You must take this step with the knee pre-flexed and braced to prevent any inadvertent rise from occurring. Do this by actually swinging your thigh rather than your foot. Knee veer must be considered; that is the knees will be closer together than the ankles. Knee veer was described in your Tango exercises. It also improves your abdominal control.

Step No. 6: Now we will discuss the drawing action itself and positioning to either closed or promenade position. When the left foot for the man (right foot for the lady) is drawn toward the standing foot the heel of the left leg is released from the dance floor and the knee is slightly higher in its position of flex than that of the right foot. The opposite is true for the lady. The inside edge of the toe retains pressure on the dance floor while the heel's position is up from the floor. Knee veer will assist this leg and foot position.

Common errors made by beginners on the drawing action include:

a) Inadvertent straightening of the knees, thus creating rise. You must avoid this fault as it spoils the Tango's feline character.

b) Releasing the foot from the floor, losing toe pressure. If you have not developed the use of toe pressure from the free foot in your dancing here is a very good place to begin! Toe pressure with the free foot (and I mean just the big toe and NOT the ball of the foot) can assist you in your balance and vertical position in hesitation movements, tucks, spins, etc. Experiment with toe pressure and it will definitely improve your overall dancing. In the case of the Tango draw, the toe pressure will assist you with timing and the amount of speed you wish to create to the next position. It will also be of benefit while you are achieving promenade position as it helps maintain your vertical axis.

c) Closing the foot too closely and too quickly to the standing foot, and continuing to move the body to the side while drawing the foot. Either of these faults can affect your partner's balance. These speak for themselves. I like to think of hugging my partner's right knee between my knees as establishing the distance of closing the knees and thighs. Develop the habit of drawing your thighs towards each

The Tango Draw

Linking one figure to the next figure with Promenade Position (PP)

other rather than your feet. This will also assist you in maintaining good toe and foot pressure with the floor.

Linking One Figure To The Next:

The last issue I want to discuss with you is the action of linking the basic position to promenade position. Diagonal to the wall (The body's plane is 45° in relationship to the wall he faces) is a common traveling position for the gentleman while moving down the ballroom floor in many dances. His partner would therefore be backing in a position diagonal to the wall. I have described these positions for both the man and the lady as a benchmark for the movement to promenade position (PP). Here is a real test for the quality of your dance frame. Regardless of how powerfully and precisely the movement to promenade position is portrayed by experienced dancers, the reality is it is a subtle and speedy movement when done correctly. It does not involve power or strength in the gentleman's lead. There are so many illusions in dance for the beginner that the feeling of correct accomplishment of a figure or position is often very different than they appear. It almost seems unfair to be tricked by your eye. Nevertheless, this is and will always be the case. Our eyes will always view the extremity and end movement. We therefore try to create the movement's end at the beginning. This happens until the coordination of eyes and feelings work interchangeably for the dancer. You must gain experience physically. Therefore the willingness to make physical error must be part of your dance learning experience. Please don't become frustrated by this fact. We all must travel this way.

I have described in the exercises for your Tango the idea of shoulders, ribs, and hips moving in conjunction with each other. This will be the essential ingredient for a successful lead to promenade position. Dancers refer to the lead as a right shoulder leading back. That will mean the shoulders, ribs, and hip rotate at once, back, to the right slightly less than 1/8 of a turn. We call this a body turn because the standing foot does not rotate. When the gentleman does this it will create approximately a quarter of a turn in his partner to the right. The man's right side and the lady's left side will deepen in their contact. The gentleman should maintain his abdominal control and thus the torque in his body while moving in promenade position. This torque will assist him in the lead from promenade to basic position as well as in creating rotation while in PP. This action on the fifth step of a basic figure or the third step of the tango draw will be known as a link to PP. In this way the dance couple can now travel from a basic dance position and figure to a promenade dance position and figure. Pattern #4 is a good example

104

of a figure that travels boldly down the floor in PP and then can be linked to another figure moving in PP.

You will also notice in the photograph of promenade position (PP) that the gentleman is facing a position between the couples' handhold and left shoulder. The lady is facing a position between the couples hands and her right shoulder. In promenade position the lady will be slightly back of the gentleman's body position. This generally produces a V like position in be couple's dance frame.

The final position of the feet in promenade and basic position:

Once promenade position is achieved, the position of the man's left foot is slightly behind the plane of his right foot. The lady however, will have her right foot slightly ahead of the plane of her left foot. This is the same as in the basic position of the Tango draw.

Rear view of couple during linking action

The Tango Rocks:

The Tango Rocks are the most versatile of all Tango figures. For beginners and advanced Tango dancers alike they are great fun to dance and a joy to have at your disposal. Tango Rocks can be used as an interlude to make your physical intentions along with your emotional intentions known to your partner; after all, that is what Tango is all about.

The variety of Tango rocks are virtually limitless once you learn to add curve or turn to them. They can take you in any direction on the dance floor. Rocks can become a pause to refresh your physical direction and to allow for new directions in your Tango to come to mind. Tango Rocks will allow you to phrase and interpret the music with greater ease. For a beginner they can become your next best friend while on the dance floor. They keep your Tango moving while you are struggling secretly for the next lead.

Choreography For Tango Rocking:

The Timing for any and all three step rocking patterns is as follows:
Quick, Quick, Slow.

Pattern 6) Left Forward Rock:

Step No.1   The gentleman will step forward onto his **left** foot.
                   The lady will step backward onto her **right** foot.

Step No. 2   The gentleman will replace his weight backwards on his **right** foot.
                   The lady will replace her weight forwards on her **left** foot.

Step No. 3   The gentleman will step forward on his **left** foot.
                   The lady will step backwards on her **right** foot.

Pattern 7) Right Forward Rock:

Step No.1   The gentleman will step forward onto his **right** foot.
                   The lady will step backward onto her **left** foot.

Step No. 2   The gentleman will replace his weight backwards on his **left** foot.
                   The lady will replace her weight forwards on her **right** foot.

Step No. 3   The gentleman will step forward on his **right** foot.
                   The lady will step backward on her **left** foot.

Man's right foot back during any Rock Step

Left foot back during any Rock Step

Pattern 8) Left Backward Rock:

Step No.1   The gentleman will step backward onto his left foot.
                   The lady will step forward onto her right foot

Step No. 2   The gentleman will replace his weight forward on his right foot.
                   The lady will replace her weight backward on her left foot.

Step No. 3   The gentleman will step backward on his left foot.
                   The lady will step forward on her right foot.

Pattern 9) Right Backward Rock:

Step No.1   The gentleman will step backward onto his right foot.
                   The lady will step forward onto her left foot.

Step No. 2   The gentleman will replace his weight forward on his left foot.
                   The lady will replace her weight backward on her right foot.

Step No. 3   The gentleman will step backward onto his right foot.
                   The lady will step forward onto her left foot.

Patterns10) a, b, c, d
L&R Progressive Rocks either Forward or Backwards

a) Left Progressive Rocks forward:
Start with Pattern 6 (The Left Forward Rock) Steps 1-3 and continue Immediately with pattern 7 (The Right Forward Rock) steps 1-3.

b) Right Progressive Rocks forward:
Start with pattern 7 (The Right Forward Rock) steps 1-3 and continue immediately with pattern 6 (The Left Forward Rock) steps 1-3.

c) Left Progressive Rocks backward:
Start with pattern 8 (The Left Backward Rock) steps 1-3 and continue immediately with pattern 9 (The Right Backward Rock) steps 1-3.

d) Right Progressive Rocks backward:
Start with pattern 9 (The Right Backward Rock) steps 1-3 and continue immediately with pattern 8 (The Left Backward Rock) steps 1-3.

Patterns 11) a, b, c, d
L&R Stationary Rocks either Forward or Backwards

a) Left Stationary Rocks forward:
Start with Pattern 6 (The Left Forward Rock) steps 1-3 and continue Immediately with Pattern 9 (The Right Backward) rock steps 1-3.

b) Right Stationary Rocks forward:
Start with Pattern 7 (The Right Forward Rock) steps 1-3 and continue immediately with Pattern 8 (The Left Backward Rock) steps 1-3.

c) Left Stationary Rocks backward:
Start with Pattern 8 (The Left Backward Rock) steps 1-3 and continue immediately with Pattern 7 (The Right Forward Rock) steps 1-3.

d) Right Stationary Rocks backward:
Start with Pattern 9 (The Right Backward Rock) steps 1-3 and continue immediately with Pattern 6 (The Left Forward Rock) steps 1-3.

The Timing for any and all three step rocking patterns is as follows:
Quick, Quick, Slow.

The development and description of the rocking action:

Tango Rocks are a three step pattern. They consist of a progressive movement on the first step, a replacement in the opposite direction on the second step, and a replacement with a very slight advancement beyond the position of the first step. As noted above, the various Tango Rocks may be preceded by a walk on either foot moving forward or backward. You may also enter any of the Rocks from the Tango draw.

Step No. 1 which is your entry to the rock figure is an abbreviated form (slightly less in progression) of a normal Tango walk. When the gentleman desires to enter the rocking action it behooves him to begin flexing into the knee and ankle of his supporting leg to create a softening action for the first progressive step of the Tango Rock. This softening should be able to be interpreted by his partner simultaneously and assist her in dealing with the body speed of the Quick counts of the first steps of all of the Tango Rocks. Additionally the Rocks must be led with a firm and controlled torso. This includes the entirety of the spinal column moving in vertical unison. A coincidental "Breathing" or flexing of the elbows, shoulders, and wrists of the leader must occur coincidentally with the flexing of his knees. This "breathing" of joints of the arms in relationship to the joints of the leg is a common coincidence in partner dancing. This will prevent an unwarranted acceleration of the lead to the lady's upper body. He does not want to create undo momentum or body flight. As we discussed in our exercises, the shoulders, ribs, and hips must move in conjunction with each other and therefore it is imperative to affect the lady's dance center rather than just her upper body. Additionally the gentleman must use the techniques of CBMP on forward left Rocks and shoulder leading on forward right Rocks. All back Rocks should use the corresponding shoulder leading technique. Both CBMP and shoulder leading were discussed and developed and your various Tango exercises.

Step No. 2 which is the replacement action of any rock step involves a slight moving of the target foot, this will prevent the body from developing too much flight or momentum and over shooting its mark. This can be a accomplished by a very slight directional movement of the foot towards the position of the alternate foot. Another important consideration would be to keep the ankles and knees sponge-like while dancing a rocking action. It is necessary for the body to be accepted willingly by the foot through the ankle so as to accomplish a thorough weight change.

Step No. 3, your concluding step of any rock action, is virtually a replacement to the position of the first step. The reason we call it a step as opposed to a replacement is that the foot is released from the floor and advances very slightly in conjunction with the direction of the rock. Very slightly means moving just an inch or two from the position of Step No.1.

If Step No. 3 is backward the footwork is ball heel and if forward the footwork is heel. When exiting the tango Rocks do not stiffen the Standing knee. It would be more desirable to move through that knee with the pre flexed position you developed in your Tango exercises.

You may exit the Rocks using any walk, including curve, if you desire. Additionally, the Tango draw may conclude this figure or any other figure you may learn. Remember in Tango a single walk is considered a complete figure. Therefore, if your Rocks end on the leader's left foot, it is completely permissible to follow with a right foot walk in either direction. The gentleman could then continue with any figure which begins with his left foot.

Turning the Rocks :

Inherent to the Nature of Tango are its curving and turning actions. I believe that the true character of Tango effervesces when a figure is done with rotation and curve. The Rocks are no different and will provide great joy when you rotate or pivot with them. Using combinations primarily made up of stationary Rocks, alternating between the left and right foot Rocks Tango dancers may rotate toward any direction.

My simple rule of body torque will assist you in your entries to rotating or turning Rocks. Examples would be:

For example the Left Foot Rock moving forward would rotate counter-clockwise after Step No. 1. The Right Foot Forward Rock would rotate clockwise after Step No. 1.

110

The Development of A Tango Amalgamation:

Let's say you want to rotate in a complete circle clockwise. The following would be true. The gentleman would complete a left foot Tango walk producing the physical logic to do a right foot forward rock. Once the vertical axis of Step No. 1 of the right foot forward rock has been completed, the rule of torque will allow you to commence and continue with clockwise rotation. Continue this rotation clockwise for as much as a half circle clockwise and conclude your rotation to complete the full circle using Left Stationary Rocks backwards. As noted above, the rule of torque will allow a backing motion with the left to produce clockwise rotation or torque. At the end of the of the Left Stationary Rock rotating clockwise, the gentleman will be over his left foot. A normal conclusion to this combination of figures would be a right foot walk forward and a Tango Draw.

Congratulations, you have just completed a 5 figure amalgamation in the American style of Tango. These five figures consisted of

1) left foot forward walk,
2) right stationary forward rock for a half turn clockwise,
3) left stationary backward rock rotating the remainder of the circle clockwise,
4) right foot forward walk,
5) the Tango Draw.

This amalgamation phrases perfectly with 16 beats of music or two complete phrases of 8.

Your counting would be as follows:

1) slow   2) quick, quick, slow   3) quick, quick, slow   4) slow
5) quick, quick, slow.

The example given above should indicate to the American Tango dancers that the construction of dance figures or amalgamations is quite easy. Figures with fancy names and many dance steps are nothing but combinations of the simplest figures in the simplest form. It is my hope that you will experiment using the figure types we have established to build a Tango that travels easily around the ballroom dance floor. A good rule of thumb would be to select a series of figures divisible in increments of 8 beats of music. In the tango a single walk can be used to phrase or to produce torque for the next figure. To assist you in phrasing your Tango, try pausing in the position of the third step of the Tango Draw in either basic or promenade position. As you become more accomplished in the usage of the foot and the head, in moving from basic to promenade position, or promenade position to basic you will enjoy playing out the drama of American Tango. The figure, the Tango Corté is also used to create pause in progression but is often influenced by a desire to demonstrate emotional interest!

Patterns 12) a & b Tango Corté:

This figure is constructed to produce a dramatic line or pose resulting from an exaggerated bend of the man's left knee having been placed behind the right leg. The actual Tango Corté consists of only two dance steps. The figure commences in closed position.

Pattern 12) a The Basic Tango Corté:

Step No. 1	The gentleman will step backward with his left foot. **Timing: Slow**
	The lady will step forward with her right foot.
Step No. 2	The gentleman will step forward onto his right foot. **Timing: Slow**
	The lady will step backward with her left foot.

Although only two steps, this figure does contain some complexity. I just wanted to warn you of this because your eyes can play tricks on you even when looking at the picture of the Tango Corté. You cannot see the weight distribution on or between the feet so pay close attention to the following. Step No. 1 is created by the man's swinging his left leg back before removing any body weight from his right foot. Make this swing of the leg as long as possible without creating any body movement. His body weight will then move halfway back to his left foot creating an even distribution of weight between both his feet. The remainder of his body's weight will be transferred to his left foot by bending his left knee approximately 4"-5" while keeping his right foot in place allowing for the straightening of his right leg. The man's left knee will be turned out from the center of his body so that it faces 90° to the left. The sequence of movements that occur between steps 1 and 2 takes place over the course of four beats of music or **two Slow counts**. Drama is created by a controlled sharp entrance and a deliberate exit. Therefore it is not desirable to pause for any extended moments. For some less athletic dancers a delay at the end of the first step could create difficulty in the approach to Step No. 2. Ladies, it is incumbent upon you to control your entire torso throughout the Tango Corté.

Step No. 2 is simply the body weight of the man being transferred forward with slight rise to his right foot so that the couple ends in close position but no higher than the elevation of your normal Tango Walks. You may want to refer to your Tango exercises relating to the elimination of rise. The lady will mirror the man's footwork, timing, and positions. This figure may be repeated and can rotate clockwise between repetitions. You may follow this figure with a Tango Draw or any suitable figure that commences with the gentleman's left foot. **Important note**: Both feet should remain in

The basic Tango Corté back on the man's left foot

contact with the floor regardless of which one has the body weight! This rule applies to both partners. This will eliminate any potential for unwarranted surprises!

Pattern 12) b The Rocks with Tango Corté:

Now that you have learned both the Tango Corté and several of the rocks, let's have some fun and combine them. Changing elevation with a Corté will aid in phrasing and add aesthetic appeal to your dancing.

This is easily accomplished by taking:
Steps 1 and 2 of Pattern 6 which are the first two steps of a Left Foot Forward Tango Rock.

Steps 3 and 4 of Pattern 12(a), which inserts the first and second step of the Tango Corté (above) as the third and fourth steps of this new amalgamation. From there repeat these first four steps and conclude with your Tango Draw. The Corté can be inserted almost at will, providing the man's left foot is free.

Patterns 13) a & b The Tango Fans:

The Lady's Fan from the Tango Rocks:

Now we will take the Left Forward Tango Rock and have even more fun with a "little attitude" by combining it with the Lady's Fan. The action of the Fan creates the drama of the eternal struggle between the sexes. This time the lady begins her cat and mouse game by ignoring him in her pursuit of him. Let's Tango on!

The Fan can be described as a swivel turn of 3/8's to 1/2 a rotation moving toward one direction and finishing in the opposite direction in promenade position (PP). The free foot will be held behind the supporting leg approximately 18 inches. Apart from the lovely aesthetic appearance, the functional reason for extending the free leg is to inhibit rise. From closed position the initial entry point of the fan commences toward what would be outside partner and then continues with the swivel to finish in promenade position. The Fan can also commence from PP. As you will soon see the fan can be done by either partner. For purposes of Quickstart To Tango we will use a closed and a promenade position fan for the lady and then an open position Fan for both partners. The Fan like, other Tango figures, has unlimited potential and variation. The entry into a Fan will always follow the rule of body torque. In addition to the Fan's

Right foot forward for lady's Outside Fan while man holds his foot in CBMP

rotation the couple may vary its direction relative to the dance floor. The gentleman will hold his leg in CBMP!

Important note: Both feet should remain in contact with the floor regardless of which one has the body weight! This rule applies to both partners. This will eliminate any potential for unwarranted surprises!

Pattern 13) a: Lady's Outside Fans

We will begin with Steps 1,2 of Pattern 6 which are the first two steps of a Left Foot Forward Tango Rock.

Step #3 of Pattern 13)a, is known as an Outside Fan, because the lady's position remains outside her partner. It will commence as a left walk back for the man and a right foot walk forward for the lady. The gentleman leads his partner to fan and to finish promenade position (PP) with him. This was described just above. Because the lady is stepping forward on her right foot the rotation will be approximately 1/2 turn clockwise to end in PP. The rule of body torque applies here (see: Rotation in Tango). The lady's head will rotate toward the direction of the Fan and then, a moment after her body has achieved PP, she will her rotate her head to PP. The gentleman must delay his lead to PP until the lady achieves perfect balance over her right foot (see: Rotation in Tango). This generally occurs at the end of the 1st beat of the slow count. The man must lead with his entire frame taking care that his right shoulder, ribs, and right hip all move in unison. The right leg of the leader is held in CBMP (see: Rotation in Tango). The Lady moves her left foot to CBMP just prior to her step onto her left foot in PP.

Step #4 is a walk forward and across in PP to finish in closed position. The feeling of this figure mimics the lady's Outside Fan. This will be approximately 1/2 rotation counter-clockwise. Carefully follow the technique of Step #3!! The couple will end in closed facing position with the legs in their normal position.

Steps numbered 5,6,7, & 8 are an exact repeat of steps numbered 1 through 4. The couple may easily alter direction counter-clockwise beginning on step #5.
Steps numbered 9, 10, & 11 conclude this amalgamation with your Tango Draw.

Conclusion of lady's Outside Fan with couple in PP holding feet in CBMP

Congratulations, you have just completed your second 7 figure amalgamation in the American style of Tango. These seven figures consisted of:

     1) Step 1,2 of a Left Forward Rock
     2) Lady's Right Outside Fan
     3) Walk in PP with swivel ending in closed facing position
     4) Step 1,2 of a Left Forward Rock
     5) Lady's Right Outside Fan
     6) Walk in PP with swivel ending in closed facing position
     7) The Tango Draw

This amalgamation phrases perfectly with 16 beats of music or two complete phrases of 8's.

Your counting would be as follows:

1) quick, quick 2) slow 3) slow 4) quick, quick 5) slow 6) slow
7) quick, quick, slow

The end of step #2
Pattern 13) b

Pattern 13) b: The Couple's Open Fan

This figure includes a variation of the basic promenade figure, a variation of the Tango Draw, and a variation of the fan that we just covered. This figure is generally met with joy by beginners as it is very demonstrative. This particular figure was used by Sean Connery and Kim Bassinger during the filming of a James Bond Movie, "Never Say Never Again" (1983).

Step No. 1   Is a forward walk in PP by the couple.

Step No. 2   Begins facing PP and ends backing in close side by side position with the gentleman having taken a 1/2 rotation clockwise. To do so the gentleman must release the couples frame with his right arm while maintaining a hand hold with his left and the lady's right hand.

Step No. 3   This begins the variation of the Tango Draw. Both partners commence Step No. 3 in close side by side position and step backward while retaining the left to right hand hold. The gentleman will be stepping backward on his left foot and the lady on her right foot.

Step #3
Pattern 13) b

Step No. 4   This is a side step taken by both partners. The gentleman steps to his right and the lady to her left while retaining the left to right hand hold. Each partner will conclude step No. 4 to the side of each other in an open side by side position with an extended arm and hand hold. The level of the hand hold will be

**Step #4
Pattern 13) b**

**Step #5
Pattern 13) b**

approximately at the elevation of each partner's sternum.

Step No. 5   Not unlike any previous steps of the Tango Draw, the free leg of each partner will be drawn to the standing leg using the previously described technique for the Tango Draw. The Gentleman is using his left leg and the lady her right. Therefore the positions of step numbers 4 and 5 remain the same.

Step No. 6   This is the most difficult step of this amalgamation. It consists of a strong step to an open promenade position of Fan for both partners. The left to right handhold must be maintained while moving to Fan position. The step to close the partners to Fan position is a diagonal step forward. Each partner will exit strongly from the standing leg towards this new position while retaining good compression in their knees. This will prevent undesirable rise and insure that the bodies maintain good vertical position. There is approximately one quarter rotation towards each other from the position of Step No. 5. The gentleman rotates to his left and the lady to her right which remains obedient to The Rule of Torque. The heads of both partners will remain facing the direction of the Fan until the bodies have concluded in a closed promenade position. At that time they will move the heads to promenade position. While this is happening the free legs of each partner will remain in Fan position, approximately 18 inches from the standing leg. Therefore the figure ends in closed PP with the legs held in Fan position.

Step No. 7   This step is a normal walk in closed promenade position by both partners. We have previously described this promenade step as a step taken forward and across in PP.

Steps numbered 8, 9, and 10 are a normal Tango Draw in closed position, preferably with rotation in a counter clockwise direction.

The timing of Pattern 13b is as follows:
1) Slow, 2) Slow, 3) Quick, 4) Quick, 5) Slow, 6) Slow, 7) Slow, 8) Quick, 9) Quick, 10) Slow, for a total of 16 beats of music or 2 full phrases of wonderful Tango music.

Congratulations, we have concluded approximately 30 variations in the style of American Tango. The use of this text will amply prepare you to dance a American Tango at any social occasion. The technique in general and specific to the American Tango will take the reader well beyond the choreographical bounds presented in Quickstart To Tango. As mentioned previously there are virtually unlimited varieties of Tango patterns available for your use and pleasure. I recommend that you use this text as a personal Tango notebook and outline, and then find a competent instructor in your area to continue your development of the American Tango. **Tango On!**

Step #6 part 3
Pattern 13) b

Step #6 part 1
Pattern 13) b

Step #6 part 2
Pattern 13) b

Step #7
Pattern 13) b